To War with The Black Watch

Gian Gaspare Napolitano

translated by
Ian Campbell Ross

BIRLINN

First published in 2007 by
Birlinn Limited
West Newington House
10 Newington Road
Edinburgh EH9 1QS

www.birlinn.co.uk

ISBN 13: 978 1 84341 032 4
ISBN 10: 1 84341 032 X

British Library Cataloguing-in-Publication Data
A catalogue record for this book is available from the British Library

Typeset by Iolaire Typesetting, Newtonmore
Printed and bound by Cox & Wyman Ltd, Reading

To War with The Black Watch

Gian Gaspare Napolitano was born in Palermo in 1907. In the 1930s he was a well-known journalist and war correspondent. In the post-war years, he published a number of successful novellas and short stories. He was also a film director and scriptwriter whose work won awards at the Berlin and Cannes film festivals. He died in Rome in 1966.

Ian Campbell Ross is author of several books, including *Umbria: A Cultural History* (Viking/Penguin, 1996) and *Laurence Sterne: A Life* (OUP, 2001). He has also published on a number of European writers, including Italo Calvino. He is associate professor of English and a Fellow of Trinity College Dublin.

Trevor Royle is a broadcaster and author specialising in the history of war and empire. His most recent books include *The British Civil War: The Wars of the Three Kingdoms 1638–1660* and *Flowers of the Forest. Scotland and the First World War*. He is associate editor of the *Sunday Herald* and a Fellow of the Royal Society of Edinburgh.

Contents

Contents

Gian Gaspare Napolitano
(1907–1966)

Ian Campbell Ross

Some writers enjoy immediate acclaim and seem subsequently never to go out of fashion or disappear from the public eye; others enjoy fifteen minutes of fame and fade for ever from view. There is a third kind of writer whose reputation suffers after his death, only for his work to be rediscovered, lost sight of and reclaimed repeatedly. The author of *To War with The Black Watch* is one such writer.

Born in Palermo on 30 April 1907, Gian Gaspare Napolitano found early success as an author and, in a life of less than sixty years, was variously known as a playwright, journalist, war correspondent, interviewer, short-story writer, novelist, television presenter, screenwriter and film director. Schooled in Verona and L'Aquila, he studied at the Military College in Rome and in the Faculty of Political Sciences at the University of Rome, but saw where his future lay from an early age. He was only nineteen when he wrote the Futurist play, *Il venditore di fumo (The Smoke Vendor)* that brought him his earliest literary acclaim, following the play's production in Rome, and later publication in 1929. By then Napolitano had already started on a successful career in journalism, having founded *I Lupi* (*The Wolves*), with Aldo Bizzarri, and editing *'900*, founded by the avant-garde writers Massimo Bontempelli and Curzio Malaparte (the latter a novelist who, like Napolitano, would subsequently turn his experiences as an Italian liaison officer into fiction, in *La pelle* [*The Skin*; 1949; trans. 1952]). Napolitano's first novel, *Scoperta dell'America* (*The Discovery of America*, 1930) opened the way for the real and imagined voyages on which he would base so much of his writing and which would lead one recent writer to dub him 'un giornalista globe trotter'.[1] Fortuitously, Napolitano was on honeymoon in Romania in 1930, when the revolution broke out that would bring King Carol II to power. Along with his wife, Maria Martone – later one of Italy's foremost literary translators, whose work included Ernest Hemingway's *For Whom the Bell Tolls* (*Per chi suona la campana*, 1946) – he reported on the situation, so making his journalistic reputation.

Napolitano's youthful success led to early opportunities for travel outside of Europe. The year 1930 saw his first visit to the Belgian Congo, as it then was, and in the following year he made a round-the-world trip that confirmed him in his lifelong love of the unforeseen and unforeseeable – in Mexico he was caught up in the cyclone that devastated Tampico, causing almost 200 deaths. In 1932 he visited Canada and 1933–4 saw him in the United States – one of his great loves – as well as back in Mexico. These trips brought forth not only journalism but also works of travel-writing and fiction, including *Giro del mondo* (1933; *Around the World*) and *Troppo grano sotto la neve* (1935; *Too Much Wheat under the Snow*). In every field of endeavour, his merits were recognized, so that he won several awards: the Premio dei Dieci for his novel, *Scoperta dell'America*, the prize of the Accademia dell'Italia for his travel-writing, and the San Remo journalism prize for *Giro del mondo* and for his long cabled report on the Tampico cyclone.

It was Fascist Italy's ill-conceived and ill-fated African campaign that marked out the following decade for the writer, not yet out of his twenties. In 1935–6, he followed the Italian army in Somalia and Ethiopia, reporting for *Il Giornale d'Italia*. Back in Europe, he found himself in Spain, sending back dispatches on the Spanish Civil War, and on the role of the Italian troops Mussolini had sent to aid Franco's rebels in that conflict. In 1939 he was a war correspondent for *Il Popolo di Roma* on several fronts. Despite this, his lack of enthusiasm for Fascism, and a desire to escape the stultifying aspects of life under that regime, combined with his love of America to drive him, in that same year, to seek a very different assignment, this time as the New York correspondent of the Rome newspaper, *Il Messaggero*.

Italy's entry into the Second World War in 1940 saw Napolitano back once more in his role as war correspondent. Already decorated for bravery in action in both Ethiopia and Spain, Napolitano accompanied Italian troops into Albania and the Balkans, this time on behalf of *Il Popolo di Roma*.

Once again he did so strictly as a journalist. A further citation for valour praised Napolitano's disregard of all danger while accompanying the army, but insisted that he went unarmed at all times, acting in the capacity of an official of the Red Cross.

After reporting from north Africa, where almost a quarter of a million Axis troops surrendered in 1943, Napolitano saw the war swing decisively against Italy. The landing of allied forces in his native Sicily in early July, precipitating the fall of Mussolini and the armistice of 8 September 1943, was the prelude to the occupation of much of Italy by German forces. Napolitano himself was in Rome in late May 1944, when the final stage of the battle for the Italian capital was raging. From the roofs of houses even in the centre of Rome, the capital's inhabitants could clearly see the artillery shelling from Tivoli in the hills to the east to Nettuno on the coast. In later years, he would vividly evoke the liberation of the Eternal City on 4 June 1944.

By the late summer of 1944, with the allied armies now pushing north towards the Germans' defensive lines in north-central Italy, Napolitano was serving as part of the Italian Liberation Corps. Subsequently, he became an intelligence liaison officer with the British Eighth Army – the same role he attributes to Lieutenant Pinto in *To War with The Black Watch*.

Giovanni Pinto – 'John' – is in every important respect a lightly fictionalised representation of the author himself.

Even the name is a barely disguised version of his own: Giovanni being the expanded form of Gian, and Pinto being the second name of his father's family who, true to the tradition of the Spanish Bourbons from whom they were descended, kept the name Pinto de Santa Elena. Gian Gaspare was still a young boy when his father died, yet the image of him he retained (or created) did much to shape his life. 'You know, I'm an old-fashioned man; I come from a military family,' a friend remembered him as saying, by way of self-explanation.[2] The older Napolitano was a career army officer, killed fighting in Africa, when his son was just eight years old. The writer would recall him with pride and affection in a number of works, including the touching story, 'Il figlio del capitano' ('The Captain's Son'), included in *Il figlio del capitano* (1958) and *Un colpo di luna* (1967; *Moonstruck*). (The latter collection also incorporates additional stories that draw on the author's wartime experiences, notably 'Il ferito borghese', or 'The wounded civilian', a tale not included in the *To War with The Black Watch* sequence but which bears an evident connection to it.) Following his father's death, Gian Gaspare – in childhood, simply Gaspare to his friends – was brought up in the town of L'Aquila, in his mother's home region of Abruzzo. At the age of fifteen, he left home secretly, taking his father's service revolver with him, to join the March on Rome in October 1922 that put the Fascist *Duce* Benito Mussolini into power.[3] An account of his journey from the Abruzzo to the Italian capital, written long after the event, does not attempt to disguise the excitement he felt – it evokes it vividly in fact – but Napolitano's disillusionment with Fascism was not long delayed. Certainly, it did not survive his first experiences with Italian forces on the Somalian front, according to an official letter written on his behalf by a government official in 1945. There it was stated that Napolitano was wholly apolitical in performing his duties as a war correspondent, and that not only were his reports free from political rhetoric but that in personal discussion he expressed his disenchantment with Fascism, revealing himself rather to be a free spirit, of independent mind, qualities that grew as time went on and his disenchantment deepened.[4]

Any autobiographical account needs to be approached with a degree of caution on the part of the reader, the more so when the writer has more than usual reason to represent himself in a sympathetic light. In factual terms, the account of Pinto's duties closely mirrors those specified in documents drawn up by the Eighth Army in July 1944. The careful wording of the letter from General Staff Intelligence to Allied units also suggests the possible wariness these units might feel about Italian officers assigned to them (something Napolitano notes in 'A place in the mess'), the letter ending with the insistence that 'Experience has shown that these officers, all of whom are carefully selected and checked, can be of great value to forward troops if their potentialities are realised'. The duties of the intelligence liaison officers were defined elsewhere as gathering information by the interrogation of Italians, according to instructions laid down by the Eighth Army; liaison between the unit to which the officers were attached and Italian units in the same area, including partisans; liaison with the civil authorities and, where necessary, with the general population; advising headquarters of any suspicious characters in the area; acting as guides in operation zones, or finding such guides (with the warning that the Italian officers would be held personally responsible for the reliability of guides they found). In the light of the tense political situation developing in Italy following the armistice, a final paragraph noted that 'the Army is non-political. Whoever has taken part in the fight against the Germans should be supported whatever party he belongs to; political discussions must be left to when officers return to civilian life'.

Life could rarely have been easy for Italian intelligence liaison officers, not simply because they had so recently been on the opposite side in the war but because secret military instructions suggested that the army's official attitude to their new allies was at best ambivalent. Among the principles distilled from allied experience in the first six months of the war in Italy, it was stated that 'Generalisations made by Italians are usually false' and that British intelligence officers should 'not expect Italian officers to be more observant or accurate because they are military'.[5]

Despite the suspicions he faced, surviving material – in the form both of official documents and personal letters – suggests that Napolitano himself gained much the same friendship and respect from his military colleagues as that which he attributes to Lieut. Pinto. Notable among these is the testimonial written by Capt. Raymond E. Legge in June 1945 (see pp. 175–76) which finally abandons its dry official tone to conclude that Napolitano would 'be assured of a hearty welcome in the homes and clubs of the B[attalion] officers should he at some future date come to England and enable us to return some measure of the hospitality he has extended to many of us'.[6]

To War with The Black Watch is a short work, yet an accomplished and engaging one, to which Napolitano remained attached until the end of his life – as his continual, if never fully completed, process of revision reveals. In the light of the author's career in film, the episodic structure of the narrative is of especial interest. That career had begun when the 28-year-old wrote a screenplay for *Passaporto rosso* (*Red Passport*), based on his personal experience of living with poor Italian immigrants in Canada in 1935, after missing his boat home to Italy – and subsequently, he co-wrote screenplays with Romolo Marcellini for *Sentinelle di bronzo* (1937; *Bronze Sentinels*) and *Los novios de la muerte* (1938; *Death's Bridegrooms*). It is clear that Napolitano thought carefully about the structure of his work, following its initial, necessarily episodic, publication in *Libera Stampa*. In later versions, the account of Lieut. Pinto's time with the Black

Watch charts the battalion's progress north from Lake Trasimeno towards the Gothic line, the Germans' principal line of defence in north-central Italy. In this, it notably anticipates a much more celebrated work dealing with the allied forces' push north through the Italian peninsula: Roberto Rossellini's *Paisà* (1946) which, in a series of separate episodes, follows the progress of the war in Italy from the Allied landings in Sicily to the Venetian lagoons. Napolitano knew Rossellini well, and commissioned music by the director's brother, Renzo Rossellini, for some of his own later work in film. Whether or not the serial publication of *In guerra con gli scozzesi* in *Libera Stampa* had any influence on Rossellini, the episodic nature of the narrative conveys with considerable immediacy the experience of war, described in 'A place in the mess' by Lord D – a fictionalized portrait of the battalion's second-in-command, Major Lord Douglas Gordon – as 'a long dull night, lit up by flashes of fear'.

Written so close to the events, *To War with The Black Watch* ran the risk of being mere reportage. Published in the war's immediate aftermath, it could equally have turned into a sentimental piece of self-justification. It says much for Napolitano's skill as a writer that he was able to give a subjective yet essentially accurate account of his time with the battalion – verifiable from the historical record and from the recollections of the battalion chaplain, Padre Joseph Grant – while avoiding the temptation invariably to place his *alter ego* centre stage. The result is a work that does not shrink from the horrors of the war, or the very special horrors of accompanying allied troops whose struggle against the Germans and their remaining Italian allies from the Fascist puppet-state, the Republic of Salò, could be won only at considerable cost to his own country and its civilian population. Nevertheless, *To War with The Black Watch* remains a constant source of engagement with questions – of personal and national identity, of courage and self-doubt, of companionship and alienation, of how men and women might find ways of living in peace in a shrinking world – that transcend their immediate occasion. The work's popularity on first publication is suggested by the fact that so much of *Libera Stampa*'s limited space was devoted to seventeen episodes, published at weekly intervals between August and December 1945.

By 1944, the 37-year-old Napolitano was fluent in English and a widely experienced traveller, familiar with many countries and peoples. Liking to think of himself as a citizen of the world, he might easily have stressed his evident ability to adapt to the changed circumstances in which he found himself, yet he remains here, as often elsewhere, something of an outsider. Friends would later find in the account of his time with The Black Watch many of the qualities they recognised in the author, not least impatience with bureaucracy and military regulations; a lack of religious dogmatism;[7] and a certain ironic detachment from his surroundings. *To War with The*

Black Watch is also shot through with a vein of melancholy that suggests Napolitano to have been at home everywhere and yet nowhere – a condition that his restless later life and career indicate may not have been far from the truth.

When the 6th battalion of The Black Watch was transferred out of Italy, Napolitano found himself attached to a battalion of the Indian Army, an experience he recounted in four further tales first printed in *Libera Stampa* in 1945. With the war now over, Napolitano resumed his journalistic career, writing for both newspapers and magazines, at home and abroad; one of his assignments took him to the southern tip of the American continent, where he reported on the Italian immigrants who had settled in Tierra del Fuego. In this, he resumed an interest in those hundreds of thousands of Italians who left the land in the twentieth century to seek prosperity in the United States, Brazil, Argentina and elsewhere. It was an interest he shared with his friend and fellow-journalist, Luigi Barzini, Jr – known outside of Italy as author of the bestselling study of the national character, *The Italians* (1964) – whose father, Luigi Barzini, Sr, a former war correspondent and reporter with *Corriere della Sera*, left Italy to found the famous Italian-language newspaper, *Corriere d'America*, in the United States. After 1950, Napolitano travelled still more widely, returning to Mexico, and visiting Brazil and Argentina, as correspondent for *Il Giorno*. The last years of his life saw him writing for the Milanese paper, *Corriere della Sera*, on a wide range of topics, including trips to Ethiopia, Japan and Paris. He also conducted interviews with leading contemporary figures from many fields of endeavour, including the philosopher Jean-Paul Sartre and the anthropologist Claude Lévi-Strauss.

Strangely perhaps, for so prolific a writer, almost twenty years elapsed between the publication of *Troppo grano sotto la neve* in 1935 and the book publication of three short novels, under the title *La mariposa* (1954). The volume – made up of 'La mariposa' ('The Butterfly'), 'Tam Tam Mayumbe' (the title derives from a funeral chant of the Mossi people of central Africa) and one of his finest works, 'La volpe d'argento' ('The Silver Fox') – offers a good indication of the geographical range of Napolitano's passions, the three novellas being set, respectively, in Mexico, the Congo, and New York. Four years later, a collection of thirty short stories appeared, under the title *Il figlio del capitano* (1958; *The Captain's Son*). The eponymous title story is the author's fictionalised and moving reminiscence of a summer spent alone with his father in barracks over forty years previously, the days passed in reading and drawing at his father's desk, and the evenings spent in restaurants, where his father seemed to treat him as an adult, never shouting at him, and even failing to notice when the waiters forgot to dilute his glass of wine with water. 'Il figlio del capitano' is a revealing story, not least for its insight into its young protagonist's unspoken fears: of the seaside, since he couldn't swim; of dogs; of the horses his cavalry officer father encourages him to ride. One line – 'Il figlio di un soldato, invece non deve aver mai paura'/'A soldier's son, however, must never be afraid' – suggests a childhood memory that the adult Napolitano took to heart in the many military campaigns in which he participated in east and north Africa, Spain, the Balkans, and in Italy itself.

It was not that Napolitano's time was wholly consumed with journalism. The interest in the cinema that had revealed itself in the second half of the 1930s was renewed and developed in the 1950s. His 1952 film *Magia verde* (*Green Magic*) – the first feature-length colour documentary on the Amazon rainforests – won the Prix International du film d'explorateur at Cannes in 1953 and a Silver Bear at the same year's Berlin Film Festival (the Golden Bear was taken by Henri-Georges Clouzot's *The Wages of Fear*). The love of distant places – at which he felt himself as much at home as in Rome – showed itself in his second feature, *Tam-Tam Mayumbe* (1955), whose cast included a young Marcello Mastroianni. Filmed on location in the Congo – a country dear to his heart on account of his long-dead father's own knowledge of it – and which he now revisited after a period of some twenty years, the film was based on Napolitano's own novel of the same name. In the same year as *Tam-Tam Mayumbe* appeared, Napolitano had also been working as an uncredited scriptwriter on King Vidor's Italian-produced adaptation of Tolstoy's *War and Peace*, starring Audrey Hepburn and Henry Fonda.

Restless as ever, Napolitano diversified his activities still further in the 1950s and '60s, working now in television. Among his major projects were programmes on New York's Little Italy; the Mayan temples of the Yucatán peninsula; the Abruzzo (where he had grown up, following his father's death); and a series of interviews with the heads of state of some of the newly independent African states.

The range of his activities, more than anything else perhaps, has been detrimental to a wider appreciation of Napolitano's writings. No further book appeared before his premature death in 1966. In the following year, a new edition of *Un colpo di luna* appeared, with over a dozen additional stories. The volume now included an affectionate memoir of the author by Luigi Barzini Jr, who took personal responsibility for ensuring the publication of Napolitano's writings, describing this to his publisher as a debt owed to a friend who would certainly have done as much for him.[8] Subsequent posthumous publications, and republications, have included *Magia rossa* (*Red Magic*; 1968); *La mia Capri* (*My Capri*, 1980); *In guerra con gli scozzesi* (1986; including three of the four stories concerning Lieut. Pinto's time with the Indian battalion), and *I racconti della dolce vita* (2005; *Stories of the Good Life*), with a preface by Giovanni Russo and an afterword by the author's daughter, Giovanna Napolitano.

Although not the author's own, the title *I racconti della dolce vita* offers an appropriate counterpart to 'Racconti di guerra' ('War Stories'), one of the section headings in the 1967 *Colpo di luna*. Nor is the title unlinked to the older Napolitano's life. In his later years, Gian Gaspare Napolitano was celebrated for combining the profession of a busy journalist with a life spent in the company of friends – and he had many – on the Via Veneto. For all the real affection for the Abruzzo[9] of his mother's family and the Sicily of his father's, Napolitano was a Roman by adoption, living in the city for nearly forty of his 58 years. Luigi Barzini would later recall that Napolitano knew everyone, and had friends from every walk of life, from writers, journalists, actors and directors to *maîtres d'hôtel*, barmen and hotel porters.[10] This world, immortalised in Federico Fellini's satirical masterpiece, *La dolce vita* (1960), finds expression in many of the stories written by their author over a period of twenty years, offering what Giovanna Napolitano has described as a picture of an entire period and its ways of life, a social analysis of Rome in the age when the city became the centre of an international film-industry social set.[11] Fellini acknowledged Napolitano's intimate knowledge of this, and the foreigners drawn to the life, in asking the author to confirm the authenticity of the foreign-language dialogue for his best-known film (a pre-production typescript of the screenplay is held in the Napolitano archive in the Biblioteca Statale Antonio Baldini, in Rome).

Gian Gaspare Napolitano is today less familiar to readers than he should be, even in Italy. Yet he was one of a generation of writers who played a role in helping to shape modern Italian fiction. In this, his role as a journalist was crucial, for he brought to his novels and short stories the same narrative clarity that distinguished his newspaper writing. The deceptive simplicity of style that characterises his best work was at odds in its own day with received notions of what constituted a 'literary' style. 'Extremely readable'[12] – the English phrase used of Napolitano's work by Emilio Cecchi, an Italian critic best known for his studies of literature in English – should be understood as a compliment, untinged with faint praise. Napolitano's prose style in fact had much in common with the early writings of Ernest Hemingway and Scott Fitzgerald. A later critic has even compared him to Raymond Carver, and if Napolitano's realism is not quite the 'dirty realism' of Carver, the brief oblique narratives that make up so much of his output suggest the comparison to be not wholly misplaced.

At the time of the author's death in 1966, many of Gian Gaspare Napolitano's friends – often themselves distinguished journalists and writers – recalled with affection Napolitano's presence in Rosati or Harry's Bar, talking from late afternoon far into the night. They remembered too the love of Scotch whisky, mentioned in more than one of the stories of *To War with The Black Watch*, and his predilection – disregarding the regimental sergeant major's preference for single malts (see p. 92 below) – for Ballantine's and, as photographs reveal, The Antiquary.[13] More perceptive or more honest than most, Luigi Barzini also recalled the almost imperceptible yet constant veil of melancholy that spread itself over the writer in his last years.[14] An exceptionally handsome man in his youth – *'davvero un bell'uomo'* as the Italians say – Napolitano's last years saw him increase so greatly in bulk that it is sometimes difficult to imagine the soldier's son who shared the hardships of military life under active service on so many fronts between 1935 and 1945. The certainty that the memory of these years remained with him to the end is particularly evident in the letter sent by a friend to the Church of Scotland minister, the Revd Joseph Grant, seeking some consolation for the writer as he lay dying (see pp. 177–83). That the Italian liaison officer was well remembered by the Revd Mr Grant is evident, not just from the words of hope he offered or from the description of him as 'a just and good person' remarkable for his 'erudition, his patience and his gentlemanly manner', but from the former padre's suggestions for small 'corrections' to the texts that indicate a perception of the journalist's concern for accuracy, even as they miss the broader poetic truthfulness at which Napolitano aimed as a writer of fiction.

Following his death on 5 January 1966, at the age of 58, Napolitano was remembered with unusual warmth in numerous obituaries and short memoirs. In his introduction to *Colpo di luna*, Barzini acknowledged the occasional unease the fundamentally liberal writer aroused in those on the left and the right. 'The fascists', Barzini wrote, 'found him too indulgent towards antifascists and reproached him for serving with the Scots of The Black Watch during the war; the antifascists deplored the warm friendships with fascists that he never denied; for those on the right he was too irreverent towards solid middle-class values; those on the left were suspicious of his attachment to the noble military virtues of former times; his praise of the former colonies; and his adolescent passion for Kipling.'[15] And yet, Barzini insisted, no one ever spoke ill of Gian Gaspare Napolitano. Despite such tensions, characteristic of Italian public life, Napolitano was a man whose successes gave pleasure to his friends, even if his failure to achieve still wider recognition and a greater degree of worldly success did not. As he wrote in 1944, describing his new surroundings among the Black Watch, he enjoyed the small comforts of life, but could do without them (see p. 173). Although his professional activities made him financially secure – though never rich – Napolitano never saw his life in material terms. The problem, he wrote, was how to write and to live – though this, he confessed at the age of fifty-two, was a dilemma he had not yet resolved.[16]

To read the work of Gian Gaspare Napolitano suggests that the problem of 'living and writing', as he understood it, was not one easy of resolution. Like the experiences of Lieut. Pinto in *To War with The Black Watch*, life was amenable to incorporation into a satisfying narrative only within limits. The melancholy of which Barzini wrote reveals itself not just in Napolitano's rendering of his experiences of battle, of military or civilian casualties, of estrangement and loss, but in his final banal meeting with the commanding officer of The Black Watch battalion. Though 'overcome with a deep, melancholy feeling of peace' at being told what he already knows – that he must leave the battalion, which is being transferred overseas – Pinto silently acknowledges that the commanding officer's attempt to speak to him on a personal level feels 'all wrong'. *To War with The Black Watch* ends, in fact, not simply with Pinto's awareness of what he and his companions have shared in their months together, but with wistful acknowledgement of all that, despite mutual goodwill, divides the Italian from the Scotsman. Whether, in the year that marks the centenary of the birth of Gian Gaspare Napolitano, and the fiftieth anniversary of the signing of the Treaty of Rome, things have changed much can now, for the first time, be left to English- as well as Italian-speaking readers to decide.

Ballykillavane, 8 February 2007

Notes

1. Giacomo d'Angelo, 'Un giornalista globe trotter', *Il Centro*, 12 April 2005.
2. Arrigo Benedetti, obituary of Gian Gaspare Napolitano, *L'Espresso*, 8 January 1966.
3. See *L'Ora*, 28 October, Anno XII [1934], 9; reprinted from *L'Italia vivente*, Anno X [1932], p. 4.
4. Official declaration by the Minister Plenipotentiary

Renato Piacentini, 5 July 1945 (Biblioteca Statale Antonio Baldini, Rome).

5. 'Instructions for the interrogation of all personnel coming from enemy territory except German PW; and for the compiling of reports thereon', 1 April 1944.

6. Testimonial letter from Capt. Raymond E. Legge, relating to Napolitano's service as an Italian Liaison Officer, 29 June 1945 (Biblioteca Statale Antonio Baldini, Rome).

7. Letter from Nicola Ciarletta to Giovanna Napolitano, 11 April 1986 (Biblioteca Statale Antonio Baldini, Rome).

8. Letter from Luigi Barzini Jr, to Count Valentino Bompiani, 23 December 1966 (Biblioteca Statale Antonio Baldini, Rome).

9. See Gian Gaspare Napolitano, *Les Abruzzes/L'Abruzzo* (Teramo: Enti provinciali di Aquila, Chieti, Pescara e Teramo, 1969), a posthumously published version of an invited lecture on Abruzzo given in Paris on 9 June 1965.

10. Luigi Barzini, 'Introduction' to Gian Gaspare Napolitano, *Un colpo di luna* (Milan: Bompiani, 1967), pp. 8, 9.

11. Giovanna Napolitano, 'Postfazione', in Gian Gaspare Napolitano, *I racconti della dolce vita* (Roma: Edizioni Studio 12, 2005), p. 156.

12. ibid., p. 9.

13. See Giovanni Russo, 'Prefazione', *I racconti della dolce vita*, p. 9.

14. Barzini, p. 17.

15. ibid., p. 8.

16. 'Il problema è per me un altro. Scrivere e vivere. A cinquantadue anni non l'ho ancora risolto'; quoted by Barzini, p. 13.

To War with The Black Watch

Gian Gaspare Napolitano

translated by
Ian Campbell Ross

A Place in the Mess

'Gentlemen,' says the captain at company headquarters, 'allow me to introduce our Italian liaison officer, Lieutenant Pinto.'

The battalion commander has just arrived from reporting to the brigadier. He is a middle-aged Scot, with a toothbrush moustache, fine, thin hair parted in the centre, a flushed face and eyes with a dark, metallic glint. He gives a slight bow, and holds out his hand to the Italian officer. A kerosene lamp shines on a table, which takes up the entire space of the mess tent.

'How are you?' says the commanding officer. 'Welcome among us. I hope you'll find yourself at home here. Are you sure you've already dined? Make yourself comfortable. Do you know everyone here? Lord Dix, the adjutant, the padre, the medical officer, the intelligence officer, the signals officer. Well, I wonder if you'll like our food. What did you say your name is?'

'Pinto, sir, Giovanni Pinto.'

'We'll call you John, if you don't mind. It will make things much simpler. The men will call you "sir". If you need anything, speak to me about it, to me or to the adjutant here, Harry. Do you know Scotland?'

'No, sir, not yet, but I hope to visit it.'

'That's very civil of you, very Italian. You mustn't expect the same from us – the same civility, that is – at least while the war lasts. The Scots talk sparingly. Don't be surprised if we don't talk to you much, especially during the early days. Do you talk a lot, on the whole?'

'Very little, on the whole.'

'Good. Consider yourself under observation, and excuse us. This evening's another business, you're a guest and a novelty. War is a very dull business.'

'A long dull night, lit up by flashes of fear,' adds Lord Dix, smoothing his fair moustache. He is the second-in-command of the battalion, and the only career officer. In consideration of his social position, the junior officers laugh.

'Your English is exceptionally clear for a foreigner,' continues the commanding officer. 'I hope you'll manage to get used to our accent, which is rather hard. We Scots are all rather hard. Do you know the history of our battalion?'

The Italian officer had read an account of it skimming through the last regimental yearbook. It belongs to an old regiment called The Black Watch, already famous for its courage at the time of Waterloo.

'We'd been told you'd be coming,' says the commanding officer, bowing politely. 'You'll find plenty to do here. It's a tricky business for us to make contact with the locals. As you'll know, it's practically impossible for the British to speak any language other than English.'

'Very difficult, anyway,' adds Lord Dix, who had studied French at Eton.

The commanding officer knits his brows. 'Yes, we've had tremendous difficulties with the French, in Tunisia and along the Garigliano, and with the Arabs and Egyptians. Everything considered, you'll be very useful to us. Isn't that true, Harry?'

'Certainly, especially with civilians who cross the lines, sir,' confirms the adjutant politely.

'During the fighting,' adds the signals officer, 'it's incredible how many civilians cross the lines during the fighting.'

'John, will be very useful to me, especially,' says the intelligence officer, meaningfully, 'to identify minefields, and booby-trapped houses.'

'And to find billets and deal with the local farmers,' insists the adjutant, stammering. The commanding officer starts to laugh.

'Perhaps you'll have gathered that we're like bears, used to living clannishly among ourselves, and every outsider who finds himself in our midst becomes a problem. We're each trying to convince ourselves in turn that we really need a liaison officer. You're the first Italian to sit in this mess since the war began,' he concludes, serious now, stroking his chin, and fixing his eyes on his guest. And again there is a silence, which continues for some time.

'I think I understand. And I hope I won't take up too much space in the mess,' says Pinto, awkwardly. Since he is a man of generous proportions, many officers burst out laughing.

'Oh, that's good! Don't worry yourself about the space. Still, you look like someone who enjoys his food, anyway,' says the commanding officer. 'By the way, you'll have to get hold of wine yourself.

'Wine?'

I'm speaking in your own interest, John. I'm afraid that you won't care much for tea and whisky.'

'On the contrary, sir. I appreciate tea and I like whisky.'

'In that case, you'll see that we'll get on well together. You'll teach us to recognise good Italian wines and we'll offer you the best whisky at our disposal. Agreed?'

'Certainly, sir.'

Lord Dix half-closes his eyes and applies himself to polishing his nails against the sleeve of his uniform.

'In any case, it will be a most interesting experiment. Almost like driving on the right.' This time, the laughter is more spontaneous.

'Do you know that in Britain we drive on the left-hand side of the road? Of course, you do. Well, you can't imagine how difficult it's been for us to learn to drive on the right, ever since we arrived in Egypt. Now that we have learned, all those millions of us British who've been in Africa and come to the continent, we should continue to drive on the right, once we're back home.' And then, point-blank. 'Were you there?'

'Where?'

'In Egypt, during the war.'

'Yes, sir, but I was on the other side.'

'Of course,' interjects the commanding officer.

'Very interesting,' continues Lord Dix, still polishing his nails, 'And may I ask you where?'

'Back and forth along the coast, I got as far as the Qattara depression.'

'Back and forth!' exclaims the commanding officer. 'Another evening, when we know each other better, we'll compare our experiences on the roads. We went back and forth a few times ourselves.' And he laughs, and with a piercing glance around invites the others to laugh. Lord Dix barely smiles.

'However,' resumes the commanding officer, 'the problem now is this, John: to do the same as everyone else. Even in this business of kilos – kilogrammes, or do I mean kilometres? – we'll have to agree once and for all. Our system is out-of-date: inches, feet and so on. Instead, in Europe, you use . . .'

'The decimal system.'

'Right, the decimal system, which is a jolly good system, they say. And when you eat pudding you use a knife and fork instead of a spoon and fork. All in all, it's more elegant – and easier at times.'

31

'At times. But we waste so much cream.'

'Oh, you've a sense of humour. That's a pleasant surprise. They waste so much cream; did you hear that, padre?'

'Yes, sir. But I'm afraid that once we're back home we'll go on driving on the left. That's what I'm afraid of, the chaplain observes, and returns to pulling on his pipe.

'And paying no attention to, what the devil's it called, the decimal system, did you say, John?'

'Yes, sir. It's a very simple system.'

'Of course, very simple. But I'm afraid that, like all simple things, it's too complicated for us. I'm really afraid, John, that it's terribly difficult for the British to become Europeans.'

'But you are a European, sir. You live in Europe.'

'Are you really sure about that, John?'

'Absolutely sure. On an island but in Europe.'

'This certainty of yours – at times, I'd really like to share it. To feel myself a European. But are we?' he asks himself, without conviction.

'I'm afraid, sir,' murmurs the padre, 'that we are only Scots.'

'Only . . . but, by Jove, that's saying a great deal. Do you understand, John, that's a great deal.'

'Yes, sir.'

'Good. My bottle of whisky, please, Taylor. And a glass for Lieutenant Pinto, if I'm not mistaken. From tomorrow the lieutenant is part of this mess.'

In a Personal Capacity

A few days later, the battalion goes to the front line, and the commanding officer announces to him that he will remain at base, with 'A' company. 'I'm sorry, old chap, you'll go the next time.' The mess is over and, in the silence, Pinto feels as though his face has been slapped. 'The men and the officers don't know you well enough yet. You could get shot, going around with that strange cap during the fighting. I'd rather that you got used to being here first.' Pinto takes his leave, walks aimlessly in the fields, finds a haystack and sits down; a cricket hidden in the hay sings in his ear. Then he thinks of Pinocchio, of the cricket by the hearth; he smiles, the sweat stops streaming down his face, he calms down. No, it's not easy, this new job.

About a hundred metres away, he makes out, through the canvas walls of the tent, the shadows of the company commanders reporting. Now he is aware of laughter, the sound of glasses, the radio passing on the news from London; then, the officers' jeep driving away into the night, towards the old farmhouses all around, scattered in the countryside and dusted with moonlight.

Reveille is at a quarter to five, breakfast at half past, and the order to advance has the march getting under way at six, but Pinto can't bring himself to go to bed. Now Taylor, the lance corporal attached to the mess, walks towards the haystack. He comes straight on, unawares, to where the liaison officer is sitting; perhaps the corporal is looking for a secluded spot. Pinto clears his throat, then coughs; Taylor stops, recognises him, salutes.

'Excuse me, sir, may I ask you if you'll take porridge at breakfast tomorrow?' Taylor is a man brimming with tact. In fact, before the war he was a waiter at the Savoy Hotel in London. Yes, the officer will take porridge, which he knows to be a sort of gruel of milk and oat-flakes, seasoned with sugar and salt. In general, the English put sugar on it, the Scots salt. Taylor advises sugar. And off he goes, in search of a more secluded spot.

The medical officer's tent next to his is open, and lit up. Its occupant, in pyjamas, is sitting at a small folding table, writing. On the night before going into action, not even the medical officer manages to sleep.

Pinto gets up and passing in front of the doctor slows down, and bids him good-night. The other peers at him over his glasses and gestures him to come in. Curious that he should have understood his need to talk. Without preamble, as though thinking aloud, he confides: 'I'd give anything for reveille never to sound tomorrow; for this night never to end.'

He takes off his glasses, polishes them with a handkerchief, puts them on top of the letter he has begun. 'I was writing a load of lies to my father.' The captain is the son of an Edinburgh surgeon. He has red hair, a face covered with freckles, and is the only unkempt officer in the battalion. One of the traditions of the mess consists of offering him, in turn, a comb to tidy up his hair. Faced with jokes like this the medical officer never reacts, and continues to eat. He is always hungry. The night before action, though, he loses his appetite, barely touches his food, is distracted, nervous, and no-one mentions his shock of hair any more. This evening, for instance, only the commanding officer addressed any remark to the doctor, asking him if the American ambulance had arrived. In answering that it had, the doctor's left cheek was shaken by a tic. No one lifted his eyes from his plate. Now the doctor invites Pinto to sit down on the camp-bed, takes a bottle of brandy from a first-aid kit, pours three fingers into an enamelled mug, passes it for his guest to drink first; then, when his turn comes, he swallows it in one gulp. He stares at the Italian's face with his red-rimmed, short-sighted eyes. The horror and the pity of war are to be read in that pale, swollen face. Then he begins to speak slowly.

'During the other war, the First World War, my father was a battalion surgeon. He returned home with his nerves in shreds after having been a butcher for four years. I write telling him that this time it's different, that we battalion doctors don't operate on the wounded any more, that we limit ourselves to disinfecting them, bandaging them, giving them a morphine injection against the pain, a penicillin jab against infection, and immediately clear them back to the first field hospital, with a docket pinned to their chest like the price-tag attached to a wooden-puppet. But maybe it's worse now that the medical officer doesn't operate on the wounded any more, that he doesn't treat them any longer. Because the trouble is that I know those puppets well. In four years, they've passed through my hands in their thousands, because you need thousands of soldiers to keep a battalion of seven hundred men up to strength. You understand?'

Pinto nods. 'The worst,' the other goes on, 'are those wounded by heavy machine-guns, the *spandau*, mortars, fragments of *nebelwerfer*. When they arrive I can barely recognise them. Just the day before they were boys coming to ask me for an aspirin, an antivenereal cream, or a laxative; they joked with me, I ticked them off and sent them away with a slap on the back. And now they're reduced to something like skinned kids. They bleat like kids. They repeat one word endlessly. "Christ", they say, or "Mum". They don't know what else to say. Rifle wounds make just a single clean hole. But now only a few get a rifle bullet, or a stray round of light machine-gun fire; they're the lucky ones. I always put on a clean gown when the action starts; after a few hours I'm red with blood from head to foot, the smell of blood gets in my nostrils and stays with me for days and days after the battle, and no amount of washing can get rid of it; it's reached the brain. And because of all this, I'm on the edge of a nervous breakdown too, just like my father. You see, I've written again this evening, to tell him that everything's going well, losses are light, the war's coming to an end; but I can't do it anymore. At times I'm seized by an urge to leave my burrow and get myself shot. This evening when the commanding officer spoke to me, even so tactfully, it was all I could do not to shout "I've had enough." And now I'll tell you why I've called you in and why I'm speaking to you like this. Because I saw your face when the C.O. told you that he was leaving you here, at base. I didn't like your face. It's not as though we were going to the theatre, and you were staying at home, is it? I mean: why force fate? Or would you be brave, by any chance?'

'On the contrary,' replies Pinto, 'I'm afraid. But I'm here and I can't accept being here if I don't share everything, the mess, the duty, and everything else.'

'You mean the risks?'

'Well, you're forgetting one thing. The army I belong to was beaten.'

'But you're a man. You're here in a personal capacity.'

'That's too easy. But when a country loses, it can't pull out and say "I'm not playing any more." You're caught up in it.'

'Right. A soldier fights. What more can he do? But now this story's about to end, don't you think it's important to put yourself back to work?'

'But it was precisely my part in the work that I was talking about.'

'Who's telling you to hang back? If they order you to do something, do it, but no more. To those boys who'll be dead, will it have helped going to bed knowing that the war's about to end? No, it will only make them more desperate if they've the time to be aware that they're about to die. Anyway, I only wanted to explain to you that no one offended you this evening. Maybe they were even doing you a favour. Don't count on receiving many more in future. And if you don't like it, go to hell,' he ended brusquely.

Pinto did not reply immediately, nor did he smile. They stood up and again drank brandy from the kit. At the threshold of the tent, they watched the moon becoming paler. To Pinto, the countryside seemed different, observed by those foreign eyes, along with his own. Who knows if the earth had the same smell as in Scotland.

The morning after, at mess, the medical officer was silent again and in squeezing Pinto's hand to take his leave, he winked.

As day began to dawn, the battalion was already on the move, with the armoured cars in front, then the scout cars, the half-tracks, the lorries full of sleepy Jocks. Then the medical officer's jeep passed by. At the threshold of the mess, Pinto waved, the doctor responding by bringing his fingers to his helmet in a regulation salute. The ambulances came last, jolting unsteadily.

'The medical officer,' Taylor observed to Pinto, putting out the mess lamp, and at the same time looking outside, 'is one of those who take too many risks. At the medical post, it's as if he were deaf to the firing.'

Buying Provisions

A new officer has arrived at the battalion. He is a 19-year-old second lieutenant from Rhodesia. The only one to be surprised is Pinto, to whom it had been explained that The Black Watch is formed along the same lines as the Italian alpine battalions; that is, by local recruitment. In fact, very few officers have arrived for some time from the regimental depot in the heart of Scotland. But the war is in its fourth year and the Guards' battalions are spread like the sun across the earth: in Burma, in France, in Egypt, in Palestine. And as each of them has suffered heavy losses in men and officers, the gaps are filled by replacements from the colonies, and especially from South Africa. The new second lieutenant is a plump, quiet boy called Michael.

He is dark, olive-coloured, with black, ox-like eyes that rest on people and objects with a calm but incessant curiosity.

'Are you Scottish?' Pinto asks, to please him. The other smiles, flattered.

'Partly. My mother's Scottish.' Mike has been in Italy for a fortnight and this is the second time he has come to Europe. He was in Italy before the war, when he was still a child. He came with all the family and has a vague, vexed memory of the endless museums, churches and antiquities they visited. The only satisfaction he had, at the end of each day, was to return to the hotel and wash his feet in the bidet. He can't stop talking about the bidet. He had never seen one before and six years later he still hasn't managed to understand exactly what they're for. They were a little too high for washing your feet. Pinto decides to leave him in ignorance.

'One of these days you'll understand by yourself what they're for.'

'I'll understand by myself. Are you sure?'

'Certain. You're a man now.'

'You mean an officer and a gentleman, as they impressed on me during the last day of training,' laughs Mike, amused.

'Exactly. And we're discussing an object that a gentleman cannot name,' explains Pinto, not without hypocrisy.

'I see.' But it's clear that Mike is disappointed.

At this point, the small truck for the provisions arrives. Mike and the Italian have been ordered to purchase provisions.

The driver is a Scot from the city, with a cunning look, filtered slowly beneath heavy, half-closed eyelids.

A hundred metres from the first roadblock there is an old farmhouse. The small truck stops in the farmyard, scattering a flock of hens.

'This seems the ideal place for eggs,' says Mike gravely.

However, the peasant farmers don't want to sell their eggs. They look at the money, shake their heads, and say no. They prefer to barter them for soap, or salt, or sugar. This is severely forbidden. Nevertheless, the Italian officer, who's in a foul mood, raises his voice and succeeds in convincing the farmers to sell twenty eggs in exchange for some tinned food. They don't want cigarettes. It's extraordinary how little value peasants place on cigarettes.

'Soldiers have already passed this way, and we're up to here with cigarettes,' explains a dark-faced woman. And she's not selling. She'd prefer soap, and holds on to the eggs. While the vehicle is leaving, the driver lights a cigarette and bawls out a kind of rhyme in Italian:

Nienti ova. Nienti gallina. Tedeschi tutto portare via.
No eggs. No chicken. Germans take it all away.

The Scottish soldier can't understand why this little song so displeases the Italian officer. He tries to smile at Pinto, to win his approval. 'There's not much to laugh at,' thinks the officer, but he can't explain what's passing through his mind.

Meanwhile, there's no longer a soul in sight. But in the middle of a meadow, behind a hedge, the driver spots a flock of geese. The meadow is on a slope and the geese run away at incredible speed, honking and flapping their wings. Every time the driver bends down to grab one it opens its short, shiny wings and flies a short distance away, slipping out of his hands. It's a kind of corrida which Pinto and Mike watch with bated breath.

Now at the edge of the field, as though from underground, a family of peasants has appeared; they watch, motionless and in silence. The Scotsman sees them, and the challenge makes him redouble his efforts; he throws himself at full stretch across the meadow and a large goose squirts out of his grasp like a ball. He gets up, furious, and goes on following the goose, that goose. Finally getting within a boot's length of it, he sends it into the air with a kick; again the poor beast, swivelling its round, maddened eye, bounces up, dazed, and, shrieking, seeks escape in the direction of the hedge; but now it's on the verge of exhaustion. The driver kicks it again, once, twice, three times, with his hobnailed boot, making a dull sound, then picks it up and panting and agitated rejoins the truck, throwing in his prey, without speaking. The goose is bleeding from its beak. The family of peasants has come up close to the hedge, and when the vehicle passes and, at a sign from Pinto, slows down and stops, a man approaches.

'How much for the goose?' asks Pinto with a dry throat.

'Nothing' replies the man, sullenly.

'Take this; I've requisitioned it,' orders Pinto, and he holds out a banknote. The other hesitates, puts out his hand unwillingly, then gathers himself together, turns his back and goes off.

'The next time,' comments Mike turning to the driver, 'don't move from the vehicle without my order.' The soldier looks in front of him and says: 'Yes, sir,' loudly, insolently.

Now they are really on the threshold of the war, the battle unfolding on the other side of the hill. The German shells are falling in the fields, in the valley, sparsely, but very close indeed.

At a small cross-roads, two MPs, seated on the saddles of their stationary motorcycles, behind the ruins of an inn, indicate they should proceed slowly, making as little noise as possible.

'Are we going on?' murmurs the driver bad-temperedly. Mike nods. He has never been in action and everything is new and fascinating to him; it might frighten him. Lifeless under the September sun, the great dark countryside soaks up the shelling. They arrive in a tiny village, which they read on a wall is called Croci. This time there is no one, only the wind making a shutter creak.

'Let's stop here,' says Mike.

The driver brings up the truck behind the wall, making a rapid manoeuvre to turn the bonnet in the direction from which they have come; he lights a cigarette, looking no one in the face. The two officers get down, and without speaking, their hearts pounding, move towards the village. Their gaze is fixed on the verge of the road overhanging the valley where seven – no eight – British and German tanks reveal themselves in sinister profile, like gallows.

Three Tiger tanks had stopped to defend the road. Five British tanks had confronted them. One of the tanks was turned over on its side, revealing its underparts like pudenda.

The one next to it had had one of its tracks broken in two, the track hanging from a cogged wheel along the verge, like guts. Three of the British tank crew, their helmets flat on their heads with chinstraps lowered, their faces burned black by the explosion, lay on the road awaiting burial. It wasn't easy to understand what had happened. At the end, perhaps, a bomb from an air attack had exploded in the midst of the group, immobilising them all in death,. Some tanks seemed intact and their crews, peered at closely through the slits, seemed like drowned corpses, their hair still alive. The bitter-sweet smell of death made their eyes run. Mike never tired of looking. Fear hasn't touched him yet, thinks Pinto. The puff of smoke alerted them in time; both found themselves on the ground underneath a tank when the shells arrived.

'We should have brought our helmets,' says Mike.

They hear bellowing now, a bellowing that chills them like a cold wind. It is coming from the house below the edge of the bank. They throw themselves down and go into the cow-stall.

A large cow lies on one side, unable to move, her belly tight and swollen, her legs rigid, pointing up in the air. A small calf jumps around her, licking her teats, calling to her softly. When it sees them enter the stall, it escapes outside, running around the well. The ox is imprisoned in the oil-press. It's impossible to see how it got into the cement hole of the press. It has a broken leg.

'There are no eggs here,' says Mike. And he goes off

towards the well, to get some water. Meanwhile Pinto busies himself with a pitchfork to bring down a pile of hay into the manger. He spreads a little next to the ox, with a bucket of water. They put another bucket of water in front of the calf, which begins to lap it with its red tongue. After maybe twenty minutes of working like this, they hear the horn of the truck sound. They leave reluctantly.

'I heard lowing, like a calf lowing,' says the driver. Mike frowns and says: 'It was an ox. A huge ox, with a broken leg, fallen into a hole. It would have needed five men and a pulley to carry it away.'

'I'll bet,' says the driver, bitterly.

He gets into gear and they make their way back at head-long pace.

'I'm almost tempted to explain the business of the bidet to him,' thinks Pinto, 'he's a real man.'

The Quartermaster's Cursing

The rain is pouring down and the quartermaster's jeep advances over the mud between two white tapes indicating the safe road, where there's no danger of being blown up by mines. The ribbons laid down by the sappers almost always follow the tarmac road, occasionally moving away from it, where the route detours around a small, suspect bridge, going into the fields, and rejoining the road higher up. The sappers work with a magnetic mine-detector, a kind of microphone grafted on to a rod which goes into motion close to metal, thereby revealing the position of the mines. They're like vacuum cleaners,' says Pinto. The quartermaster captain gives a weary smile.

'The trouble is,' he explains, 'that the last pressure mines laid by the Germans, the anti-tank mines, no longer have metal covers, but wooden ones. The mine-detectors no longer work, you have to use your eyes.'

The Q.M. is one of the oldest officers of the battalion. He was in the campaign in France and, during the retreat, he was dug in for three days at Dunkirk, waiting to embark. It was then that his hair turned white. He shows Pinto a photograph of himself in the summer of 1939, showing him to have been a thin young man in bowler hat and spats, leaning on a walking stick.

'Were you a student?' asks Pinto.

'An accountant.' And as the wind carries the smoke from a burning haystack towards the jeep, the Q.M. starts to swear beneath his breath. 'Fucking smoke,' he mutters, 'fucking smoke.'

The countryside is deserted. Beneath the rain, the flames of haystacks fired by the retreating Germans, that have burned throughout the night like torches, die waveringly away, changing into smoke as dense as ink, that catches at the throat with its stench of corpses.

After a couple of hours' travelling in convoy, infuriatingly slowly, first passing a lorry or two, then marking time behind a tank, or queuing before a temporary bridge, they arrive at the position where the battalion has made a bridgehead, as it's called, on captured ground. The Q.M. disappears into a large tent. It is no longer raining, and the sky has cleared. A short distance away, among the ruins of a house, two civilians, one in a railwayman's uniform, are kneading a small quantity of flour on a table.

'What are you making?' says Pinto, politely.

Hearing themselves addressed in Italian, the men jump as though bitten by a tarantula.

'Piada,' replies one, and explains, 'the bread from Romagna.' The other turns his head and moves away, searching among the ruins. He digs with his hands, and in the soil finds a still-intact earthenware plate, a small mirror, a cracked mug. He is the one dressed as a railwayman.

'It was his house,' says the man kneading the dough. The other turns and gives a frightened smile. A smile sadder than weeping. Pinto would like to ask if there is someone who remains buried under those ruins, but doesn't dare.

'Luckily,' explains the man, 'we had all escaped to the river, the women and children and the rest of us. We hadn't even managed to make it under cover when the house received a direct hit.' While Pinto speaks with the two civilians, the Q.M. reappears at the entrance to the tent and indicates that tea is ready.

The tent is a kind of refreshment post for officers newly arrived from base – replacements. There are also camp beds, where some men are sleeping, while others, stretched out, stare at the roof and listen to the rain which has started to fall again. Pinto sits on a camp-bed and drinks his tea. Then, from his haversack, he takes a pair of socks and leans forward to unlace his shoes. His feet are soaked, he sneezes and inveighs in a loud voice.

'Fucking rain,' he says.

'Agreed,' sighs the Q. M., while a young lieutenant, with straw-coloured hair, bursts out laughing. 'John curses like one of us,' he exclaims.

'Oh, the British don't curse,' says Pinto. 'I mean, they hardly ever curse. They swear. That is, they don't take the saints in vain. At most, in extreme circumstances, they invoke Christ's name. Only Catholics curse seriously.'

'Do you mean that Italians know how to curse and the British don't?' asks the lieutenant, cut to the quick.

'No. It's too hard to explain. It's that the swear words the British use are monotonous, and that's where their strength lies. In their lack of imagination.'

'Well, I must say,' murmurs someone in the shadows, 'we still have something to learn.'

'It's not that,' says Pinto, getting entangled. 'You've discovered the power of two or three expressions that, when repeated to the point of exasperation, give a sense of the boredom, the monotony, the fatality of war. One is the word Cambronne used. You make enormous use of it in the army. A four-letter word.'

'John, I forbid you to repeat it,' says the Q.M. reddening.

'I won't repeat it, but I have to listen to it the whole day long.'

'Well, the fucking thing I'd like to know, since we've got to this fucking point,' explodes a lieutenant, who up to that moment had been lying down, with his eyes closed, pretending to sleep, and suddenly sits up on the bed, 'is when this fucking rain is going to stop. Sunny Italy, eh? Then you'll explain to me what that fucking expression means, won't you John?'

And quickly he puts on his camouflage waterproof and leaves the tent.

'Well, I'm not sure there's anything left for me to explain,' Pinto concludes. And everyone laughs, louder than necessary.

As for the captured positions, they consisted of a small hill beside a church, a tiny village called San Patrignano. The Scots, who had led the assault on these heights, found themselves under fire from six-barrelled German mortars whose shells, arriving together with a noise like a pulley, explode like a Catherine-wheel: *nebelwerfer*. For its part, the battalion suffered losses in excess of a hundred: twenty-five dead and the rest wounded. The battalion behaved very well in this action, very probably more than one of them will be decorated and the result is that the men are in a foul mood. They are in a foul mood because of their dead comrades, their wounded comrades, because of the terrible suffering that accompanies fighting, and they are in a foul mood because it's raining, and they can't even wash their clothes.

Pinto leaves the tent and goes down the hill to the road where, beneath the rain, a long column of refugees is driving ahead of it the animals saved from the German raids.

'Where are you coming from?' asks the liaison officer. An old peasant stops to explain that they had taken refuge on the slopes of San Marino and that now the battle is over they are returning home. The others walk on in silence. From the hill of San Patrignano, one can see, behind a veil of rain like frosted glass, the coastal towns: Riccione, Cattolica, Rimini, with the lines of hotels, clinics, and villas, large and small, empty like shells. The battle has just reached Rimini, and the immensely tall, dense, monstrously heavy cloud of smoke, unfolding across the sodden countryside like the wings of a gigantic bat, reveals that a large petrol store has been hit and is burning just outside the city.

'The Greek brigade is fighting in the Rimini suburbs now,' says the battalion's second-in- command to the Italian officer who, standing at the road block, divides the crowd of refugees, with the help of a couple of MPs, into two files, one on either side of the road.

'Follow the tape and keep the middle of the road clear.'

Barefoot, two nuns were coming up the muddy road. The older one was holding the hem of her robes with her left hand, and with the other, clasping to her breast the sandals she had taken off. Her companion with bare feet, very white on the sopping ground, was walking a little ahead of her. But in her right hand, high above her head bound in starched linen, this nun was carrying a crucifix instead. Walking on up the road, she turned around from time to time to shout: 'Come on, come on, Sister Teresa, we're almost there.' Small, minute, black, with those smooth white feet in the mire, she seemed a swallow carried by the wind in the midst of a storm.

'Do you need anything?' asks Pinto. The nun doesn't even look at him. 'Nothing, nothing,' she murmurs, and walks on.

Crossing the Savio

The battalion had already crossed the river. Not all the battalion, and not all the river. One company was on the other side, along with another company of Royal Fusiliers. The fusiliers were from another battalion. This operation, in technical jargon, was called a bridgehead. So now there was a bridgehead across the river, and the men who had 'set it up' were fighting furiously to 'widen' it. The Germans, for their part, were struggling to 'eliminate' it. In consequence of this cold military terminology the men of the battalion were moving from one house to another, like mice, under German bombardment. At this point, it was necessary to 'reduce the pressure' on the bridgehead.

Two tank officers and eight men arrive at battalion head-quarters. They are looking for a ford across the river. A reasonably shallow ford, with a gravel bed – such, in fact, as would allow tanks to cross to the other bank.

All this means that a foot patrol, just a few men, must search for a fording place in the river by themselves. At this point, the Italian liaison officer says, 'all right', he'll look for the ford. He has heard from the partisans this morning that the ford does exist.

'Do you mean, John,' says the battalion information officer, 'that you're willing to accompany the patrol?'

'Yes, sir, I'm willing.'

'John,' says the colonel, 'I must make it clear that you're not bound to go.'

'I'm very sorry, sir, but I feel myself obliged to go.'

It's clear that everyone is expecting this reply, but the fact that John has given it immediately is a relief for them all.

'Call me "Lofty",' says the higher-ranking tank officer. 'Give up calling me "sir" and call me "Lofty"; this other friend of ours is called "Dick".'

There are two officers – a major and a lieutenant – and eight men, six tank crewmen, a sergeant and a corporal. They have light machine-guns, Verey pistols, coiled ropes, rubber waders up to the groin. They go down towards the river, among the trees, noiselessly. On the ridge behind them are the heavy machine-gun placements. The bursts carry over their heads, whistling, intermittently, one after the other. The Italian doesn't remember exactly where the partisan who offered to find the ford this morning lives. Two or three attempts, going on all fours into the shelters dug into the river bank, come to nothing. Finally, he finds an old man who knows the river, knows the ford, knows that it's no more than 70 cm deep, served in the other war against the Austrians, is afraid of nothing, wants to come – and in this way they arrive at the river. It is a river swollen by the recent rains, clear and rippling. It flows by murmuring, barely whispering beneath the moon. Four men remain where the shingle ends, going down on one knee and removing the safety-catch of their light machine-guns.

Now the small group walks into the mud. The old man stops, points to the water, and says: 'The crossing is here.' He explains at length that they have to go straight, and then run parallel to the opposite bank, but that he can't go into the water because he has rheumatism. 'I'm always ready to do my duty,' he says, 'but pneumonia's pneumonia.' He speaks loudly, hushed to no purpose by the officers. He will wait there.

'Have you understood properly?' says Lofty to the Italian officer.

'I think so.'

And they go forward into the mud, making a dreadful noise. In fact, they are probably making very little noise, but those five men who are still going forward feel their ears roaring. Instinctively, they look towards the bridgehead, towards the battle that is going on perhaps five hundred metres away, looking towards the red bridge, and the reddish flickers of the battle. The other bank, in the stretch immediately in front of them, is silent, enigmatic. They hear the sound of a car in the distance.

'Jerry,' says the Englishman, 'that's Jerry.' Which means 'German.'

All of a sudden, the small patrol is caught in the beam of a searchlight. It is scarcely more than a passing phosphorescent light, behind which their outlines dissolve.

'It's a rotten business,' says Lofty, 'a rotten business.'

The rotten business consists of the fact that they have wet feet, and now wet knees. The current is strong, the stones on the bed become loose underfoot. They can't find the ford. They have to try further down. They have to try again. Until all of them sink into the river; some up to their chests, some swimming, one carried away by the current. All of them swear beneath their breath; they swear frequently, until the group joins up again and goes back.

'I'm sorry,' says the old man on the bank, 'I'm really sorry, the river has risen.'

'There's nothing we can do about it,' says Lofty.

'We'll have to try again at dawn,' says the other officer. He is small, bulky, obstinate; he hasn't opened his mouth until now.

While they are returning, the wrath of God is unleashed. Everyone is firing, Germans and British. They hear the civilians shouting with fear in the shelters. The searchlights suddenly bathe everything in light. An artificial moon. They light up a temporary bridge over which, 600 metres away, tanks pass in silhouette, like ghosts.

'What a waste of effort,' says Lofty. And he takes hold of a bottle of gin offered him by the sergeant. Reunited now, the eight men and three officers stand up under the trajectory of the fire, amid the mewing of stray bullets.

'Give me a swig too,' says the Italian officer.

The Empirical Major

Major Elms is a living example of British Empiricism applied to military regulations.

The major, who is limping as the result of a wounded foot, has refused a month's leave in England. He came back to the battalion as soon as he was released from hospital in Perugia, on the eve of the action. Such attachment deserves reward. So the commanding officer held on to him, reconfirming his rank.

'For a moment,' the major explains to Pinto, 'I was afraid I'd go back to being a lieutenant.'

'Pinto had heard tell of the acting ranks of the British army many times, but doesn't dare confess to having understood very little of how they work. So, to get the subject going, he observes that, according to him, Major Elms would, at most, have been reduced to the rank of captain.

'Oh! my real rank is lieutenant,' replies the Major, and once again, to Pinto, it's as clear as mud.

'To keep the rank of captain for the duration of the war,' continues Elms, 'you have to have held the higher rank for at least three consecutive months. I was named company commander with the rank of major eighty-six days ago. I still have three days to go to reach three months. I was wounded two months ago and another officer immediately replaced me. And since the number of majors in a battalion is fixed and I found all the places filled, I risked going back to being a captain and therefore a lieutenant. Seems clear enough, doesn't it?'

While Elms is speaking, Pinto thinks that he has never seen anyone wear a uniform better.

At twenty-six, Elms doesn't just look like a major, he is the very model of one: he speaks, gestures, has the manners, the grooming and the moustache of the senior officers. Even a slight stammer, giving him an opportunity to think before replying, confers maturity on his speech. And yet, if he had been obliged to go back to being a lieutenant, Pinto would have been present at an apparently convincing transformation. Elms would have given up the silk kerchief around his neck, his visible watch chain, and even perhaps, who knows, his generously proportioned moustache, while his manners, now grave and affable, would have assumed the modesty appropriate to a junior officer, and his speech would have returned to being rapid and concise.

'Meanwhile, even though I'm ten or more years older than him, I'm still a lieutenant,' concludes Pinto, and is aware of experiencing a feeling very akin to envy.

'There's one thing I haven't understood very well,' he says aloud.

'What's that?'

'Well, given that the number of majors in a battalion is fixed, how did the commanding officer manage to keep you at the rank of major?'

'Ah,' explains Elms, blushing and not without tripping over his words, 'that's easy. He kept me here at base in reserve, without putting me back on the battalion strength. There's always a need to . . . er . . . to reorganise the staff officers after action. Almost certainly I'll go back to commanding a company. However, in three days I'll be a captain.' Pinto batted his eyelids, a trifle dazed.

'And you, have you never been a captain?' enquired Elms, politely.

'Never. For us to be promoted you need a decree.'

'Of course, I was forgetting. 'What a strange army!' concludes Elms, frowning.

The Wine Scandal

This time the mess is a real room between walls, with a roof over the officers' heads, a floor under their feet and windows at their backs. Much better than a tent. This is what the officers at headquarters keep on saying, especially when it rains. The autumn rains have begun, and the liaison officer is held personally responsible.

'You told us that the good weather would last throughout September, John,' repeats the colonel, knitting his brows.

'I'm very sorry, sir, I didn't say that, only that generally the weather is good in September.'

'I suppose that now it's begun to rain it will never end. Or am I wrong?'

'There are sure to be many good days, even before the St Martin's summer, sir.'

At this point, the conversation becomes totally entangled. The liaison officer tries in vain to explain the length and consistency of a St Martin's summer, having recourse to the Americans' 'Indian summer'. Finally the conversation is interrupted by the corporal attached to the mess, who appears, rather embarrassed, on the threshold.

'What's up, Taylor?' asks the colonel.

'The farmer, sir.'

'What farmer?'

The farmer who owns the house, sir.'

'And what does the farmer want?'

'To speak to the Italian officer.'

'Why does he want to speak to him?'

'That's what we can't understand. It seems to be about the wine, sir.'

'If the farmer wants to speak to the Italian officer it's really because you and the rest of us can't manage to understand him. But first or all, what's happened to his wine?'

'It's rotten wine, sir,'

'We'll see about that. But how do you know?'

'Hem, hem. The men drank a drop of it, sir.'

'You're one of the men too, aren't you, Taylor?'

'Yes sir.'

'Bring the farmer in.'

'Very well, sir.'

'John, this is your business,' mutters the commanding officer, rather embarrassed. 'In so far as you're the liaison officer it falls within your duties to have contact with the civilian population and listen to their just complaints. In so far as you're a member of this mess . . . well, decide for yourself.'

The farmer, whose house it is, is a rather small man, with untidy hair and a pepper-and-salt beard. Every morning he goes to search out the liaison officer in front of his tent, to tell him what the Scottish soldiers had done to him the day before. At the beginning, everything was a disaster. The Scots began by taking over the kitchen and two bedrooms. Bit by bit he found himself in the cowhouse, with his wife, three grown-up children and two cows, and with the entire house occupied by people who treated him as an intruder, when he wasn't actually being arrested by the sentries.

'It's raining,' the liaison officer explained to him, 'and the soldiers can't keep getting soaked all the time. On the other hand, only the officers and the cooks are sleeping in the house. Have you made friends with the cooks?'

'It's difficult. I can't speak the language.'

'My batman doesn't speak the language either, and yet he's made friends with the cooks, and with the quarter-master-sergeant.'

And so, bit by bit, the farmer begins to get on with the Scots.

'You've got to imagine that you've got a battalion of alpine troops in your house,' the Italian officer explains to him. These men are tough fellows as well, but they're good-hearted.'

And so the farmer has begun to get supplies of tinned food, sugar, flour and evaporated milk. His wife and daughter wash uniforms, shirts and socks all day, asking to be paid in tinned meats and jam. But now, dealing with the question of wine, it's another matter altogether.

'First of all, John,' says the commanding officer, 'ask him how long there's been wine in this house. Didn't the Germans drink it all?'

'Three days ago,' explains the farmer, 'I trod the grapes. And now the soldiers are drinking the fermenting must. You'll understand, I'm very worried. Drinking the wine like this is the same as taking a purge. If they feel ill, then it's not my fault. But the fact is that they don't want to listen to reason, and I can't make myself understood. They think I mind about the wine.'

'Tell the truth: you do mind.'

'I'm sorry, but I don't want to be held responsible.'

While Pinto is explaining the whole story, the commanding officer exchanges meaningful glances with the medical officer, whose face is rapidly darkening, taking on by degrees a ruddy flush that rises from his collar to the roots of his hair.

'That's where all the dysentery is coming from,' says the commanding officer, making himself ill with laughter. 'When I think that the doctor here has forbidden them to drink water from the well.'

'It would have been simpler to forbid them to drink bad wine.'

'I really don't know what's happening to me,' says the doctor at this point, getting up in haste, 'I must have caught a stomach chill. Would you excuse me a moment?' And he rushes off.

'A rather mysterious flight,' concludes the commanding officer, 'truly mysterious.' And he bursts out laughing again. The farmer looks at him and laughs as well, without knowing why.

Sunday Morning

'I'd like to marry a girl who'd never speak a word to me before I'd finished my breakfast,' comments the signals officer aloud, slowly sipping his last cup of tea. (The last cup at breakfast, naturally.) The signals officer, or 'Signals,' hasn't even finished speaking when he begins to blush. He has caught the padre's eye, and today is Sunday. Besides, 'Signals' is the youngest officer at headquarters and the junior lieutenant. He should never speak without being spoken to. At least, this is what the second-in-command, Lord Dix, thinks. The Italian officer who had begun to laugh good-humouredly, feels his blood freeze in his veins. Scotsmen with empty stomachs are better left alone. They don't speak, they grunt. And then today is Sunday – the Sabbath, that is – and everyone is in melancholy mood. The Scots will be thinking of home, they will pen minute airmail letters, special one-sided letters, letters that will be photographed in a line one after the other and sent on a roll of film to England, and on north, to their beloved Scotland, their old, green land of curling rivers.

On Sundays, the padre is the first to rise from table. He has barely touched his food, in order to prepare himself spiritually for the sermon he will shortly deliver. Through the open window, in the morning air, the group of officers still gathered around the table can hear the peremptory tones of the RSM, the Regimental Sergeant Major, the senior non-commissioned officer of the battalion, and in a sense the highest authority after the commanding officer. The RSM is presiding at this moment over the very important manoeuvre of unloading the tiny field organ from the padre's jeep. The padre rises at this point, and gravely inquires of the commanding officer whether he is disposed to attend divine worship.

This is one of the most solemn hours of the week, when a battalion of soldiers of the British army reverts to being a Scottish religious community, a congregation of the Church of Scotland.

The battalion has already gathered in a semicircle in front of the field organ. Two sermons will be delivered this morning, to thank God, to praise him, to ask his forgiveness for the sins of the battalion, to invoke divine protection on the battalion: that of the padre and that of the commanding officer. The colonel accordingly rises to his feet, wipes his moustache, damp with tea, straightens himself, and the Italian officer clearly sees tradition enter into him, and possess him whole. He sees this extraordinary fact: the spirit of Scottish tradition; the spirit of the ancestral clan take possession of a twentieth-century man, and pervade him. At this moment the commanding officer is a priest and the regimental padre, God. Immediately afterwards, all the officers leave the mess, one after another, behind the commanding officer, who is suddenly possessed by tradition as by the Holy, or the Evil, Spirit, since to the Italian officer, as a Catholic, it seems a little of both. He is admiring, respectful, and disturbed; and much taken up with hiding these feelings of his.

Only the signals officer has remained in the room, watching the other officers move off, with a dog-like gaze. He gets up, comes over and puts a hand on the shoulder of the Italian who, standing at the window, observes the ceremony taking place in the farmyard.

'John,' he says, 'are you ready?'

'Ready for what?'

'To come to mass, John.'

'But I never go to mass, Ray.'

'John, but aren't you a Catholic like me?'

'I am a Catholic, an Apostolic and Roman Catholic, and that's why I never go to mass.'

'Ah, John, you're a bad Catholic. You must go to mass on Sundays; it's a duty.'

'You're right, I'm sorry, I was forgetting, let's go to mass.'

Naturally, under arms, mass is a duty: a duty preceded, in the British army, by a meticulous church parade.

On Sunday morning, all the soldiers, freshly shaven, washed as well can be, with spats and belts freshly blancoed, submit themselves to church parade. Now the Scots sing, to

85

the sound of the field organ, played by the clumsy fingers of the padre. They sing a hymn, a Scottish hymn beginning 'Onward! Christian soldiers'. They sing with grave voices, all together, officers and men. The Italian officer and the signals officer go out into the farmyard and hurry towards the half-destroyed church of San Patrignano, whose bell, which has remained undamaged in the battle, has continued to summon the faithful. The Catholic brigade chaplain is there, awaiting the Catholic soldiers, in order to confess them, give them communion, say mass, speak a few words of homily and sing a hymn or two with them.

The signals officer isn't the only Catholic Scot in the battalion; there are three other officers, company officers, and about fifty of the men, at once Scottish and Catholic – Catholics who have managed to remain so, through the centuries, from the time of Mary Stuart.

Even the Italian officer senses this, and an irresistible force leads him to put his right hand through the signals officer's left arm, in a moment of religious solidarity. The signals officer, slightly astonished, looks at the Italian officer, and timidly accepts that manly embrace. And the two of them, together with the men, march towards the half-destroyed church on the hill, in front of which the slightly surprised and pleased villagers have already converged. 'Is this, then, God?' the Italian officer asks himself. 'God, are you here?' And God is with them, and with the Scots behind them, and with all men, on Sunday morning, after the battle.

Conversation in a Dug-out

The first wave arrived while the liaison officer was standing in front of the villa, trying to convince the owners that the battle wasn't over yet. At a certain moment the *nebelwerfer* made themselves heard. A wail sounded in the air, like the siren of a monstrous vessel approaching, sailing through the skies.

'*Katyusha*' shouted the owners of the villa, and disappeared.

'So much breath saved,' thought the Italian officer, having meanwhile spotted a dug-out, a hole cleanly cut at the foot of a haystack. There had been no need even to measure the distance; he found himself inside and he was fine. He had landed on something soft, or so it seemed.

'Excuse me sir,' a voice said in his ear, a deep baritone voice, 'but could I take my leg out from under your chest?'

The officer was on the point of standing up in confusion when the *nebelwerfer* began to fragment all around the hole. They were like Catherine-wheels, one was always exploding just when they seemed to be spent. During this time, the Italian was clasping tightly to himself none other than Mr Wilson, the RSM himself.

'They're a nasty sight, sir,' said Mr Wilson, 'a nasty sight, these *nebelwerfer*.'

'Nasty,' said the Italian. 'And I'm sorry if I landed on top of you.'

'You landed on top of me only because I got into the hole before you. But an old soldier, sir, doesn't need to hear the whistle to spot the smell of a bazooka.'

'What did you call it?'

' "Bazooka", which is the same as *nebelwerfer*. And what do you call the damned thing?'

'*Katyusha*.'

'You see, there's always way of making ourselves understood. Who knows what *nebelwerfer* means?'

'Fog-thrower, I think. It's a kind of self-propelled mortar which can fire gas canisters if need be.'

'Extraordinary things our friend Ted thinks of. Do you like my name for him? Ted. Not Boche or Kraut or Jerry. I call him Ted, short for the Italian *tedesco*, which I think's best of all. Who knows what I'd do without good old Ted at the moment. This is a good hole, for instance, one of the best I've ever been in – deep, narrow, just what you want. Well, you can see straight-off that Ted made it: a good solid, durable job . . . Dear Ted, my old friend for five years now.'

'Five years of war, Mr Wilson?'

'Going on six. And always with this regiment and always with the "socks"; there are only a few of us old ones left – those who were at Dunkirk, for instance. There would be

Gian Gaspare Napolitano, 1907–1966 (Courtesy of
Giovanna Napolitano and the Napolitano Archive,
Biblioteca Statale Antonio Baldini, Rome)

Gian Gaspare Napolitano and his wife, the translator, Maria
Martone, in 1930 (Courtesy of Giovanna Napolitano and the
Napolitano Archive, Biblioteca Statale Antonio Baldini, Rome)

Gian Gaspare Napolitano (left) returning from the US and Canada in the 1930s (Courtesy of Giovanna Napolitano and the Napolitano Archive, Biblioteca Statale Antonio Baldini, Rome)

Gian Gaspare Napolitano on board a troop ship bound for Albania in 1941 (Courtesy of Giovanna Napolitano and the Napolitano Archive, Biblioteca Statale Antonio Baldini, Rome)

Letter relating to Gian Gaspare Napolitano's service as intelligence liaison officer with The Black Watch, 29 June 1945 (Courtesy of Giovanna Napolitano and the Napolitano Archive, Biblioteca Statale Antonio Baldini, Rome)

Rome, 29/6/45

As Intelligence Officer of the Battalion to which Gian Gaspare Napolitano was attached as I.L.O. I would like to pay some little tribute to his valued assistance.

In Nov. 1943 Gian joined the Battalion and within a very few days had rendered us valuable assistance in many directions.

The information which he sought unceasingly from civilian sources proved invaluable in the location of enemy booby-traps, mine fields and tunnels in the river banks by which German patrols had frequently gained access to our lines, information which was to prove an important factor in the ultimate capture of the River Montone line.

Later in the Battle of Faenza and again in the Central Sector we were greatly indebted to Gian for the difficult and trying task of evacuating refugees and civilian wounded from the front line, often under conditions of extreme danger, for the interrogation of prisoners and the thousand and one tasks that fall to the lot of an I.O. Throughout this period Gian had become so much a member of the Battalion that it was with sincere regret that we learned that he was to return to civil life, but he can be assured of a hearty welcome in the homes and clubs of the Bn. Officers should he at some future date come to England, and enable us to return some measure of the hospitality he has extended to many of us.

Raymond E. Legge. Capt.

Gian Gaspare Napolitano bound for Albania, 1941
(Courtesy of Giovanna Napolitano and the Napolitano
Archive, Biblioteca Statale Antonio Baldini, Rome)

The first episode of *To War with The Black Watch*, *Libera Stampa* 19 August 1945. Subsequent episodes were published under the title *In guerra con gli scozzesi* (Biblioteca romana dell' Archivio storico capitolino, Rome)

Gian Gaspare Napolitano, directing his prize-winning film *Magia Verde*, in the Amazon rainforests, 1953 (Courtesy of Giovanna Napolitano and the Napolitano Archive, Biblioteca Statale Antonio Baldini, Rome)

Gian Gaspare Napolitano, with Italian actress Anna Magnani, Rome 1958 (Courtesy of Giovanna Napolitano and the Napolitano Archive, Biblioteca Statale Antonio Baldini, Rome)

Gian Gaspare Napolitano on the Via Veneto, c. 1960 (Courtesy of Giovanna Napolitano and the Napolitano Archive, Biblioteca Statale Antonio Baldini, Rome)

about twenty of us who could tell about Dunkirk. The padre was there as well. I was a sergeant then.'

'And how old are you, Mr Wilson?'

'First of all, I know I'm 27 years in the army, and I started off as a drummer-boy, at 13. Twenty-seven and 13 make 40. Or am I wrong? Do you want to see Master Wilson?'

'With pleasure.'

'Pull yourself a bit further down; rest your back against the slit-trench wall, cross your legs, pull your helmet well down on your head, because Ted's starting up again. He's mad about having had to leave the villa. Have you seen the empty bottles we found in the living room this morning? An incredible number. Now I can open my jacket and pull out my wallet. And here is Mrs Wilson, and Miss Wilson, and here's Master Wilson. Now you know the whole Wilson family. What do you think?'

'Wonderful children, Mr Wilson, wonderful children, plump, round, fair-haired, blue-eyed.'

'Just like their father, sir, just like their father. Can I offer you a cigarette, sir? All in all, it's not bad here once you get used to it. Do you like British cigarettes, sir?'

'Very much, and American ones.'

'Yank cigarettes. They're like Yank whiskey. There's only one whisky in the world, sir, and that's Scotch. How I'd like to be at home, sir, in the pub with a good glass of whisky in my hand.'

'Whisky and soda.'

'Whisky and water.'

'Whisky and soda with ice.'

'Sir, permission to tell you that whisky doesn't go well with soda, and is never drunk with ice. The Americans, colonials, maybe even the English do it, but not a Scot. Give me a good glass of whisky, really tasting of smoke, a glass of whisky with at least five years in cask, a glass of whisky from my own village. Have you ever heard tell of McDonald whisky, sir?'

'I've never heard the name, Mr Wilson.'

'That's how you foreigners are when you think you know about whisky. You talk of Black and White, Johnnie Walker, Antiquary, John Haig, Ballantine's, Teachers, and you don't know McDonald, the whisky from my home village.'

'That's enough of that talk, Mr Wilson; otherwise I'll want a drink.'

'And what about me then? I want a drink so much, I'd make do with a glass of wine, even though I don't really like it.'

'Mr Wilson, you talk about whisky and I'll talk about wine. What do you know about wine?'

'Nothing, sir, you're right. But maybe, sir, we can get out of here. Apart from the fact I've broken all my bones; Ted's given up firing. Put your head down, he's starting again. Still, it's been very pleasant meeting you here, sir, very pleasant indeed.'

Padre Grant

'John,' says the commanding officer, 'the padre needs a rest. The padre is tired, and he's seen too many unpleasant things these last few days. I'm putting him in your hands; take him to Florence and have him visit lots of churches and lots of museums. He's the only officer in the battalion who really enjoys things like that.'

'Very good, sir,' says the liaison officer. And he salutes without clicking his heels. Clicking your heels in the British army is thought very bad taste.

The padre is the battalion chaplain – in civilian life, the Revd Joseph Grant, a minister in Scotland. He lives in the manse at Grantown-on-Spey, Morayshire, Scotland. He lives in the manse of Cromdale. Under arms, he's the padre, Captain Grant.

The unpleasant things the padre has seen in the last few days are dead soldiers from the battalion. At war you try not to look at the dead. The padre is the only person who can't do that or, even if he could, wouldn't want to. The padre lays out the dead, buries them, honours them, watches over the battalion war cemeteries, writes to the families of soldiers who have fallen, been wounded or are missing in action. After the battle, the padre counts his boys, and weeps, in his heart, for those who are no longer there. But he cannot weep with his eyes, only in his heart. He is a fairly young Scottish minister, thirty-nine, married, with a wife who is a children's doctor, and two young children. He is a smiling, elegant minister, who doesn't wear a dog-collar, nor even a chaplain's cross on his uniform. Only his flashes are different, purple instead of red. At mess, he puts up with the officers' jokes and is forgiving if anyone swears in his presence. He is a good chaplain, always back and forward between one company and another, in his jeep. And he is a good officer, the padre; an officer with no fear for his own safety, that is. But he is afraid for his men; for them he has pity and compassion. Only he cannot weep, because weeping is bad for the troops' morale.

Everything considered, he is happy to go to Florence and says so to John, who is sitting beside him, carefully driving the jeep. At Riccione they have to stop to say hello to Archie Callander, a major in the battalion. Only Archie is dead, and now rests in the allied cemetery behind the hospital. He passed away not two days ago, says the nurse.

Archie's grave is a small mound, next to a line of small mounds, and all are covered with flowers, because it's the 2nd of November.

'Who put these flowers here?' says the padre to the Italian

officer. The Italian passes on the question to a peasant farmer working in a field nearby; the peasant is digging and has stopped to look up with one foot on the spade and the spade in the earth.

The farmer is a little embarrassed.

'We did,' he says, 'we put them there. Today is, All Souls, the Day of the Dead, we went to the cemetery to take flowers to our dead, and then we came here.'

Padre Grant knits his brows, as he does every time he doesn't understand something. From the jeep he has brought a white wooden cross carefully painted, in white, with the rank, name and date of birth of Archie Callander. So the officer learns that Major Archie Callander was twenty-five, and was born at Grantown-on-Spey, the town where the padre is minister in civilian life. Now the liaison officer explains to him the Italian custom of honouring the dead on one special day of the year and the padre smiles. The peasant sees the furrows disappear from the brow of the foreign officer, and smiles as well.

'Thank him, John,' says Padre Grant.

'But why?,' replies the farmer, 'Why thank me? They're a few wild flowers. We've treated these men like our own dead, that's all.'

'Thank him again,' says the padre, 'Ask him to lend us the spade.'

The padre carefully digs a hole, for the new cross. The cross with the battalion crest and the letters R. I. P.

Requiescat in pace. Now the padre stamps on the upturned earth all around the base. The farmer crosses himself.

'When it rains,' says the farmer, 'the earth goes down. But I always put it back.'

'Thank him properly, John,' says the padre.

'Don't worry yourselves, it's as though they were Italians,' says the farmer, 'just the same.'

And he begins to tell how he was in the war, not this one, the other one. When the padre tries to give him something he refuses, and goes away, shaking his head.

'Pay for the flowers we bring for the dead?' he says, scandalised, while he begins to till the soil again, shaking his head.

'Archie Callander, do you remember him?,' says the padre, while he gets back up into the jeep and puts it into gear. 'Do you remember him well?'

The Italian remembers him, with his brown hair and dark eyes, and his smile, and his medal, that he wanted to stay in the army after the war and become a regular; he remembers it all.

'Do you remember when he came to play poker one evening, and won all the time?' says the padre.

'How shall I tell his mother?' he starts again in a low voice, still looking at the road. 'We're neighbours in Scotland, and the Callanders are one of the leading families in the village. Not gentry, or anything like that, but a good family. When Archie was a boy, a student, and came home on holiday, I took him with me to fish for trout. We went down into the river, where the level's low, the water's clear, and you can see the stones, and there are holes, and he wore rubber waders up to the groin. How shall I tell his mother?' And he keeps on looking at the road, and then, suddenly, smiles. 'I was back in Scotland,' he says.

The Battalion Enjoys Itself

The day the commanding officer received the Distinguished Service Order, or D.S.O., he went to lunch with the brigadier. He returned quite exhilarated by good whisky and formally promised the officers at headquarters that he would stand them drinks, in great style, as soon they found a proper occasion.

From that moment on, the organisation of the party passed into the hands of the second-in-command, Lord D. The battalion was resting, but it could be called into the line at any moment. It was therefore necessary to act quickly and decisively, in line with regimental tradition. Lord D. accordingly set himself to work, and for three days the officers had a hell of a time of it.

First, Lord D. got hold of the field telephone and ensured the participation of the most senior and the most fashionable officers in the division. When he was sure that a couple of generals and the brigadier would come, things – from that point of view – began to go as smoothly as if oiled. Lord D. was a career officer educated at Eton and Sandhurst and was, above all, Lord D. Where he had no family connections, the fascination of a centuries-old name came into play. The commanding officer of the battalion, who in civilian life was a great mill-owner, followed the manoeuvres of Lord D. on the telephone with fascination and deep embarrassment. Everyone said yes. Within a short time, the officers' quarters were filled with electricians, flowers and bottles containing an entire month's ration of beer and spirits. The participation of the divisional light orchestra was secured in double quick time. The furniture of the quiet provincial apartment led an infernal dance. A large bedroom with an alcove was transformed into a dining room; a piano was hoisted from the road by means of ropes, and squeezed into the living room through the window. The officers recalled their regulation dress kit from base: kilts in the regimental tartan came out of mothballs and for two days were to be seen hanging at the windows, inducing wide-eyed stares from the good people of the town who, naturally, had never seen so many soldiers showing off their skirts. For three days the mess cooks worked feverishly to prepare the daintiest titbits, and Taylor, the lance corporal who had been a waiter at the Savoy in London, who would be charged with presiding over the bar, was severely reproached by the second-in-command because he had addressed him as 'Your Lordship,' instead of 'sir'.

'You must excuse me, sir,' said Taylor gravely, 'but I really thought myself back in the old days.'

Lord D. was certainly a good soldier, tough and decisive in combat and a great swearer of oaths in difficult moments. But his voice, which rang out roughly and peremptorily in commands, knew also how to turn gentle and persuasive when the moment arrived to put into action the worldly social graces of its owner. It was a singular voice, modulated like an organ, educated but never affected, without the shadow of a Scottish accent in conversation in the mess, but which knew how to become Scottish at any moment Lord D. held such a concession to be opportune, whether speaking familiarly with the troops when at ease or in combat, or when the great moment arrived to tell some anecdote with a peculiarly Scottish flavour to it.

The evening of the party found Lord D. in the act of arranging flowers in the vases of the room prepared for the entertainment. Lord D. knew, as few others did, the art of transforming a middle-class house into an elegant British officers' club.

In fact, he was just putting the final touches to the flowers, when a young officer, conveniently placed at the foot of the stairs, came in hot-and-bothered to announce the arrival of the divisional commanding officer.

'Ah, Dick's here!' said Lord D., restoring the necessary calm to the colonel with a glance. 'Dear old Dick!' and shaking the colonel's hand, moved graciously towards to the highest divisional authority.

General H. used to play polo with Lord D., in India. As for his aide-de-camp, he was Lord D.'s cousin, a mere baronet.

And so the great battalion party began. The entrance of the general coincided exactly with that of the plates of sandwiches in the reception room. After the first greetings, followed by the faintest embarrassment, Lord D. asked the general what he would prefer to drink. The general would only drink beer, and from that moment on things went swimmingly. The commanding officers of the other battalions in the regiment, glancing around with furtive attention, made rapid estimates to themselves of the value of the drinks lined up behind the bar, of the flowers, and the lighting (obtained from batteries provided by the divisional motorpool) and concluded to themselves that never, ever would they have been able to furnish anything of the kind. But naturally the Scottish regiment was older than theirs, and tradition explains a great deal. It certainly justifies a rather exorbitant mess bill at the end of the month. The meal proceeded in relative silence: everyone was speaking quietly to his neighbours, and comments on the hand-painted menu were soon exhausted. A moment before the toast, however, the pipe-major in person, enormous, resplendent in his traditional uniform, entered the room, playing the regimental charge at the top of his lungs, and, still playing, made a complete turn around the large, astonished table, before presenting the pipes to the colonel.

The colonel, paling, uncorked an old bottle of port, ready for the occasion, poured a generous glass, and handed it to the pipe-major, who was standing rigidly to attention.

'Your health!' said the pipe-major, and drank it off in one go.

Jimmy McDonald

During the battle for the 'C' bridgehead, Captain Jimmy McDonald called on the field telephone to say that he had found a barrel of beer left behind by the Germans, and that he, of 'B' company, intended to drink it all, down to the last drop. The battalion commander found himself on the south bank of the river, overhanging the river itself, in a villa surrounded by a large park of firs that ran right down to the shingle, the villa itself being hidden among the trees on the hill.

The voice of Jimmy McDonald arrived clear and cheerful in the telephone room, first of all provoking envy among the operators.

'A barrel of beer!' said the signals sergeant. 'Oh, lads! A whole barrel!'

And the soldiers licked their lips, dreaming of at least a glass of that beer. The news reached the colonel who was just worrying about the men on the other side of the river – the men who constituted the bridgehead, Jimmy McDonald's men who for the past two hours had shown no sign of life. The signals lieutenant entered the room where the colonel was nervously consulting an ordnance map.

'Well,' said the colonel, 'that bridgehead?'

'Things are going well, sir. Jimmy has telephoned just this minute.'

'Be more precise. Is the bridgehead strengthened?'

'I think so, sir.'

'What do you mean: "I think so." That's the second company I've sent across the river. What I want are facts,' said the colonel, rolling his eyes.

'The fact is, sir, that Jimmy has found a barrel of beer.'

'A barrel of b . . .'

'Yes, sir.'

'Tell him to consider himself under arrest. No, in fact, I'm coming and I'll speak to him. Call him on the set. A barrel of beer, and I'm on tenterhooks. Only Jimmy would have the nerve.'

'Yes, sir.'

So the radio operator called Jimmy on the set.

'Hallo,' he said, in a sing-song voice, 'Hallo 02, hallo 02, this is CL calling. Over! CL calling 02, CL calling 02! Over! Reply to my call! CL calling 02! Over!'

At this point the cavernous voice of Jimmy McDonald was heard distinctly.

'Hallo GL, this is Jimmy speaking! Over!'

'Hallo 02! Hallo 02! Jove wants to speak to you! Over!'

'Hallo, 02, this is Jove speaking. Where are our friends! Over!'

'Hallo, Jove, this is Jimmy speaking! Over! Our friends have run off and they've left me the beer. Over!'

And here Jimmy told the story of his mission on the other side of the river. How he had crossed the river on the ruined bridge during the night; how, once on the other bank, he and his men had found themselves framed in the sights of the *nebelwerfer*. And how, to get out of his difficulties, he had attacked the first house on the other bank with grenades, from all sides simultaneously, the main door, the door into the garden, and even from the roof – because they had managed to send a small unit of men with tommy-guns on to the roof, and, after the attack had begun, these men had removed a load of tiles from the roof and sprayed the single-storey house with bullets. It turned out that the house was the headquarters of the German rearguard, and that all the Germans who weren't dead or wounded had been taken prisoner. He hadn't been able to make radio contact before now because the Germans also had a set of the same type and as soon as they had crossed the river it had caused interference. What should he do now?'

'Nothing,' said the colonel. 'Nothing. Have you lost many men?'

'Five,' said Jimmy McDonald. 'McKinley's dead.'

'Poor McKinley,' said the colonel. 'And how are you?'

'I slipped on the roof and scraped my forehead,' said Jimmy McDonald.

'You slipped because you're too fat,' said the colonel with

glistening eyes. 'That's what you are, fat, and you've got bandy legs. Drink the beer now!'

'Your health, sir!' said Jimmy McDonald.

And they heard his laugh. The laugh of Jimmy McDonald, small, fat, and bandy-legged. The best drinker and best soldier in the battalion.

Sixteen Crosses

What has happened to make things so different? The second-in-commands of the companies remain at base, along with the quartermaster and five or six lieutenants. There is also a major who walks with the aid of a stick and in the mess sits in the C.O.'s place. But no one laughs anymore, or speaks aloud. News has leaked out that the battalion didn't even reach the front line before they were already up to their necks in trouble. Three officers slipped away to fill the places of three other subalterns fallen in action. The whole thing is taking place less than ten kilometres away but it could all be happening on the moon. The officers continue murmuring: 'May I have the salt, please?' 'Of course.' 'Thank you.' 'Pass the mustard, please.' 'French or English?' 'French.' 'There you are.' 'Thank you.' 'A drop of milk?' 'No, thank you.' And so on. If it weren't for the intermittent rumbling, no one would pay attention to the aircraft passing back and forth in convoy over the clouds like lorries going to unload refuse on the outskirts.

The day after, the padre arrives to order sixteen crosses from the battalion carpenter, a sergeant, and then they know the extent of the losses. The dead almost all belonged to the same company of rifles: mown down by heavy machine-gun fire while they were attacking a hill near Coriano.

For the first time, Pinto hears that name that will, in the history of The Black Watch, become synonymous with the name of a battle in the Italian campaign. The carpenters prepare sixteen crosses painted white, each with the regimental crest. The chaplain works to put the dead men's pay-books in order. Above each one he stamps the phrase 'Killed in action'. Then he writes sixteen letters, one for each family. He sends for Pinto, of whom he has a request to make. The Revd Grant, doctor of divinity, minister of the Church of Scotland, tells Pinto that the fallen men almost all come from his own county, men from the valleys around his own village, on the banks of the River Spey. He has written the letters by hand, in his neat, tiny handwriting, always using the same simple and compassionate expressions. Then he goes out to superintend the loading of the field organ on to his small truck. He is preparing to return to the front, where he will give burial to the dead and honour them with a final service. And since two of the dead are Catholics, it would be appropriate that Pinto should pray for them. That was why he had called for him. 'And for the other fourteen?' Pinto would like to ask, but looking at that face, baked by the sun, the eyes sunken from lack of sleep, the inclination passes. Apart from anything else, would he still know how to pray?

He retires to read under the tent, forcing himself to nurse his book, to lose himself in reading as in a dream when his batman comes to ask him if he could have a word. It's about a peasant in one of the farmhouses. He wants to speak to the Italian lieutenant. Since the two of them arrived in Romagna, the batman, Francesco Cocchi, is livelier than usual. His eyes shine, he grooms his long fair hair with greater care, he cleans his teeth persistently. Cocchi now sleeps in a haystack, together with a family of peasant farmers.

He has found a way of getting his lieutenant's laundry washed by a good-looking girl.

'Is something happening to you?' Pinto says to him, to tease him. 'You're more cheerful.'

'It must be because we're closer to home and I can speak dialect.'

'It seems to me you've found yourself a sweetheart.'

'Well, my sweetheart's not too far away.'

In fact, Francesco Cocchi is from Reggio Emilia.

The farmer's wife, still in charge of her household, is waiting for the lieutenant with a bottle of wine in her hand. The bottle is sealed with wax, and the woman waits for the lieutenant to taste the wine and tell her what he thinks of it. They sit opposite each other, and the woman pours the wine. The wine is good. While the officer drinks, the woman looks at him attentively, judges him, weighs him up. She is small and plump, about fifty. She holds her hands, deformed by toil, on her lap; her eyes are beautiful, black, deep. Behind her, around the spent hearth, her husband and a group of men feign indifference.

'How are things going?' asks Pinto, attempting to give her back the glass. The woman fills it up once more, hesitates, then says slowly: 'They're not too bad. I wanted to ask you: is it certain that the Germans won't come back?'

'Certain. Why?'

'Nothing. Just that before leaving, the German warrant officer who was sleeping here said they'd be back. And now people say they're coming back.'

'Who says?'

'People.'

'What people?'

'Oh, people. People who pass by on the road, evacuees fleeing the battle. But if the lieutenant says that it's not true, so much the better. The important thing is that the war ends quickly.'

'So far as you're concerned the war's finished for good. The battle's passed you now.'

'Where have they got to, these people you're with?'

'I'm not allowed to tell you, but in any case I don't know. How has it been for you?'

'Well, they took all our basins. A lot of chickens and eggs and a calf. But we're left without a basin to wash our faces. Is that right?'

'And didn't they give you anything in exchange?'

'Nothing. They took them, and that was that.'

'And you've no tinned goods, shoes, allied blankets, cigarettes, soap. Are you sure?'

'Oh, they gave us a few things.'

'Be careful. Tinned stuffs, chocolate, cigarettes, sugar, coffee, those you can keep, but not sell. But don't let yourselves be seen going around with allied blankets, shoes, or uniforms, especially military-police ones, those with the red berets, otherwise there'll trouble for everyone and months in prison for the men. Hide them well. Like you did with your girls. Where have you hidden the girls? Not that I want to know. Do the same with the stuff. Do you understand?'

'I understand.'

'The bicycles, too, hide them well, in the straw, in the attics, until after the redcaps have come. Then you can go around with them again. Understand?'

'Yes, sir.'

'How much is the wine?'

'That's free. Where is the lieutenant from?'

'From Rome. Why?'

'Just curiosity. Do they pay you well?'

'Like other Italian officers. Why?'

'To know why you do this job. Meaning no offence to the lieutenant, your batman says you don't have to do it.'

'And yet I do have to do it.'

'At least the lieutenant is an honest sort and not a liar like his batman.'

'Well, now you know it, stop worrying. And thanks for the wine.'

'It was the only thing we could do. We unearthed it specially for the lieutenant. We felt sorry for you, not even having a drop of wine.'

Pinto goes back towards his tent. A peasant has brought out his plough and oxen and is working in the fields. 'How's it going?' the lieutenant asks him, as he passes close by. The other stops the animals.

'The earth's become harder, They flattened it with the lorries, with the tanks. It's as hard as stone.'

'Take heart.'

'We've plenty of that.'

Private Francesco Cocchi of Reggio Emilia, class of 1918, follows Pinto like a soul in torment.

'What is it?'

'Lieutenant! I've heated water for you to wash yourself.'

'Thank you.'

'Excuse me, lieutenant, but you made me look really bad.'

'Keep a hold of your tongue. Those people were right.'

'The lieutenant was joking. But those people can't understand the lieutenant.'

'In fact, they understood me very well. I really needed a drop of wine.'

'Yes sir.'

They arrive at the tent and Cocchi carries out the tripod, the bowl, the sponge, the towel. Pinto takes off his jacket, folds up his sleeves. Cocchi pours the warm water over his hands.

'Where did you heat the water?'

'In those people's kitchen.'

'Do you think they go to church?'

'They'll go, all right. But I couldn't guarantee that they're religious. You know that in these parts they don't have much time for priests. But, excuse me, why are you asking me this?'

'Well, for Padre Grant. He asked me to pray for the dead of the battalion, the Catholics. Then I thought: who knows if I couldn't ask them, to remember them in their prayers.'

'I wouldn't do it, if I were you, sir.'

'Why?'

'Because everyone has their own dead.'

'The dead are dead. I mean . . . they're all equal.'

'But not the living, sir. These have so many dead, in Russia, in Libya, in Albania and in the bombing raids. Without counting those the Germans killed. The people are poisoned. But you could always try asking the women.'

'Maybe it's too soon.'

'That's it, sir, it's too soon.'

I Belong to Glesca

Major Shaw belonged to Glasgow, and Glasgow belonged to him. At least, this is what the chorus of his favourite song said. The major sang it every evening after he'd been drinking a little, which meant that he sang it every evening, so that even the Italian liaison officer had ended up by learning it.

The Italian officer had a clear, ringing voice, but every now and then, when things seemed to be going well, he went out of tune.

'What's the matter with you, John?' the major would exclaim. 'Have you never heard of bel canto?' He said *bel canto* in Italian, thinking he would please Giovanni Pinto.

'I belong to Glesca, dear old Glesca toun,' the major began.

'But there's something the matter wi' Glesca, for it's turning roun' and roun'' he went on, and enjoyed himself hugely because Pinto was forcing himself to imitate a Scottish accent.

'I'm only a common wee working chap,' the song proclaimed, 'but when I've a couple o' drinks on a Saturday, then Glesca belongs to me!'

The strangest thing about the whole business was that Major Shaw didn't come from Glasgow at all. But it was just as though he'd been born there, having spent his adolescence and early adult years in the city.

The liaison officer, for his part, had never been to Glasgow. Nevertheless, by dint of having heard it spoken of, he had ended up by knowing it: dark, dirty with coal dust, the great quays shining beneath the rain, and the cobbled streets, and the great tarmac road that led up to the hills above the city, the hills where the great houses of the rich were to be found. It was an ugly, comfortable city, the major explained, with its little pubs, where you drank two sorts of beer: ale, clear and refreshing, and stout, black, heavy, good for singing.

Small bars, full of light and smoke – at night, real little islands in a city at first foggy, then rainy – beneath whose signs the coal dust shines in the cracks between the cobblestones. And the docks full of ships from every land, loading coal. 'A friendly city, in fact,' he explained.

'In a city like that, sir,' said the Italian one evening, when they had had begun to know each other a little better, 'I'd end up dying of gloom.'

The major looked at him in surprise, then smiled and said that he understood his point of view.

'It's not that I enjoy myself all that much in Glasgow either. But it's like an ugly woman who's got under your skin. Now I belong to that damn city.'

Major Shaw was a tall, large, robust and courageous man,

decorated with the Military Cross, his flesh ruddy like roast-beef, and given to sudden rages. He wasn't a career officer and didn't come from an old family, but he never found himself embarrassed, like the other officers from modest backgrounds, when faced by Lord D. It was clear that the two officers didn't get on too well. There had never been any real friction between them, just the odd verbal skirmish, a difference of opinion expressed politely but with more than necessary decisiveness. Enough, in any case, for it to be understood that the two didn't much like each other.

Major Shaw hadn't finished university and this was his secret cross. But his father had died while he was studying at Edinburgh and he had been forced to start work before he had expected to. However, between the ages of eighteen and thirty-five – that is, up to the eve of the war – he had had time to accumulate a small fortune, enough to be able to realise his ambition of going to live in the hills above Glasgow.

'Between the ages of eighteen and thirty-five. That means you're forty now, Major Shaw.'

The major was sipping whisky and, half-closing his eyes, nodded agreement, without speaking.

'From the age of eighteen to thirty-five makes seventeen years, am I right?'

Once more the major indicated his agreement with a nod, and from his lips came a satisfied murmur, like the sound of a cat purring. In fact, he had a cat's grey eyes.

'And you were in Glasgow all that time?'

Major Shaw stared at Pinto a little surprised at so much insistence and shook his head. Then he began to speak. 'I've been around,' he said. 'In the East, you know, Hong Kong, the China Seas, the South Seas, a commercial agent, a merchant, an employee, an accountant' .

Nothing else. Pinto understood that he was pleased by the questions but he couldn't manage to confide in him. Only once did he allude to his dead wife, who was buried at Shanghai. Like others, he passed the time reading and smoking. He had read an enormous amount of books, and continued to read them – in his tent, in the mess – without apparent profit.

'I never remember what I've read. I wasn't made for ideas, I want facts, but reading helps me pass the time, it calms my nerves.' And straightaway he'd plunge into his reading, as though ashamed of having said too much. He was waiting for the end of the war to go back to Glasgow. Once – it was in September 1944 – he asked Pinto if he thought the war would go on much longer.

'In my view, we're almost at the very end,' Pinto replied.

'Really?' said Shaw. And he looked at Pinto with interest, before lowering his eyes to his book.

Major Shaw hadn't much to do. He now commanded 'S' Company – 'S' for Support. It was a unit formed by open-topped half-tracks that carried Bren guns, and assault and anti-tank weapons, ideal for manoeuvring in support of infantry on flat terrain, or in the desert. In Libya, 'S' company had been employed a great deal, as it had been in Flanders. But since the Italian campaign had begun, it had had few occasions to see action. For this reason time never seemed to pass for Major Shaw. But he hadn't moved a finger to alter his fate because, in war, this brings bad luck. One morning, however, he appeared in the mess more cheerful than usual, whistling the same song as ever. The commanding officer of a company of rifles had been wounded and Major Shaw had been ordered to replace him. Because of this he was leaving the battalion mess and so he had come to take his leave. He said goodbye to Pinto, who said jokingly that he would come and look him up in Glasgow. He also took his leave of Lord D. who had signed the order of the day with his transfer. He took his leave and thanked him.

Major Shaw died three or four days later, during the capture of Cesena. A burst of machine-gun fire hit him just as he had succeeded in reaching the perimeter ditch of the airport with the first platoon. The liaison officer saw him arrive on a stretcher at the medical post, covered by a bloodied tent-cloth. The major's blood ran from beneath the stretcher on to the ground.

'They got me,' he murmured to the Italian with a smile, 'They mustn't have liked my face.'

He was pale and stank of death. The medical officer indicated to the stretcher-bearers to put the stretcher down on the ground, and the major died while they were giving him a morphine injection. Pinto would have liked to tell

Shaw that the war was over for him, and that he would be going back to Glasgow, but he didn't manage it in time. Shaw was still smiling, and his brave soldier's smile hardened in death. It was as if he had never existed and in the mess no one spoke of Major Shaw. Then one evening some new officers arrived and sang 'I belong to Glesca'.

'Poor Major Shaw!' murmured the Italian.

The embarrassed silence that greeted his words told him that he had committed an indiscretion. Speaking of the dead in the mess brings bad luck. But after all Pinto was a foreigner and couldn't know how to behave himself properly on every occasion.

A Story About Civilians

The first civilian casualty was shouldered as far as the road from a path along the shingle of the River Savio. The house was tall, and you arrived by means of a short-cut through the trees covering the hill overhanging the river. Every now and then, an artillery shell or a shower of *nebelwerfer* arrived, smashing the trees or knocking their tops off. Six labourers took turns, panting under the poles of the stretcher. Behind came a regimental policeman with a light machine-gun, the Italian officer and the son of the wounded man, who coughed because he was consumptive.

The wounded man had been hit at the beginning of the battle, while he was standing at the door of his house, a short distance from the river. His family had waited for three days before deciding to ask for help from the Scots, and even then, it was a neighbour, an agitated partisan with a tricolour armband, who brought the news.

'John,' said the commanding officer to the Italian lieutenant, after the partisan had told his story, 'we must do something for these people.'

The wounded man was old and had had his skull opened

by a shell-splinter: thin, watery blood seeped from the wound on to a pillow now soaked with the liquid; the skin of his face was grey, like that of a man already marked by death.

'Why didn't you come before?' the Italian officer asked the members of the family, just to say something; but even as he spoke he felt it was pointless. The old woman didn't even reply; she looked at him, through her tears, as if she was looking at some object.

'We couldn't move,' said the son. And then he told him that he was consumptive. He also looked at the officer with a sullen gaze that expressed fear and bitterness. And the officer understood what that look meant: it's your fault, the fault of everyone in uniform, that my father is dying.

The second casualty lived in a shelter dug into the river bank, in the damp, springy, coffee-coloured earth. Three or perhaps four hundred people had left the city, fleeing the bombing raids, and had lived for months now in those holes. The second casualty was also an old man, and had been hit in the groin. Horrible as the wound was, the man talked volubly, joking with his wife and daughters. To put him on the stretcher, the officer, the stretcher-bearers, and the group of Italian partisans had had to enter the shelter on all fours. The wife of the wounded man, a tidy, dried-up working-class woman, bore the intrusion with great embarrassment. That those men, those foreigners should see her wretchedness: the heap of stones and the iron plate where she cooked *piada*, the bread of Romagna, her few saucepans, the miserable provisions, the rolled-up blankets and mattresses, the piled-up clothes. She embraced her husband, with a tenderness born of long and modest familiarity, while fighting back her tears. The officer waited until the farewells had been completed, then all together, with the stretcher they clambered up the high bank towards the road. The Germans on the other side of the river opened fire, a shot sank angrily into the pliant earth, perhaps fifty metres away. The stretcher-bearers left the injured man on the path and ran to hide themselves behind a bush. After a while they returned with downcast eyes, took up the casualty again on their shoulders and regained the road.

The following day a boy was injured in the hand. So the commanding officer ordered that the civilians should leave their holes.

The Italian officer went back outside of the holes to talk to the families. He distributed a few sweets to the children, cigarettes to the grown-ups, and gave his little homily.

The extraordinary thing, the officer was thinking as he was speaking, and telling them they had to get away, that it was dangerous there, and that in the refugee camp they would have everything for eating and sleeping and milk for the children, is how good these people were, how willing to believe in something, how polite they were, how resigned . . . too resigned. And he took care to explain, to convince, to smile. And he was ashamed of what he was doing.

They left the day after, in four groups, all with a bundle or a suitcase in hand. A few men obtained permission to stay behind to guard their belongings. Poor belongings, poor riches.

This time, there was no sign of the Germans. When everyone else was in the lorries, a tiny old woman arrived last, in tears, literally in the arms of the liaison officer. Just as the lorries were leaving, the Germans opened fire but fell short. The little old woman crossed herself and said to the officer: 'You're a good man, you're very good!'

The officer turned away and began to walk towards the villa serving as headquarters. He was ashamed of himself, a dumb sense of irritation was coming over him. When he arrived at headquarters, everyone was packing their bags.

'The evacuation's complete, sir,' he said to the colonel.

'What evacuation?'

'The evacuation of the civilians from the river, sir.'

'Thank you, but there was no need. The Germans are retreating, they're heading off, *alles kaputt*,' said the colonel.

The Battalion Moves Off

At a certain point, the Italian liaison officer had to recognise that it's very difficult to pretend for long not to know what's going on. Not knowing what's going on in wartime is called 'security' and the British are extremely adept and extremely well-trained at this game. This time, the matter in question was not knowing that the battalion was moving off, was leaving Italy in fact. Knowing, and showing you know, a detail of this kind can be very dangerous in wartime, precisely with regard to the security of the army in general.

Yet the signs were obvious: the battalion was moving off. The officers were destroying or getting rid of the biggest encumbrances from their kit, as is usual on the eve of a long journey – one of those journeys, in the case in point, in which the dimensions and weight of personal kit are no longer flexible affairs, subjects for discussion, but are established by precise instructions. The officers returned their extra blankets, gave away books or magazines, or gave cumbersome field furniture – seats, armchairs – to colleagues in other divisions, destroyed correspondence and paid their arrears in the mess. The regimental numbers and divisional colours were carefully scraped from the vehicles, and the outlines painted over, manifest proof, this last, that the battalion was not destined for a period of rest at the rear but was preparing to go straight to another front, to leave Italy, to get ready for a sea voyage.

Not all the battalion officers were aware of their new destination; those few and more important ones who were behaved with some embarrassment in meetings with the Italian officer, as befitted their status as men in the know. First of all, they were all very considerate to him. Considerate, on great occasions, as only the British know how. All at once, they seemed to be consumed by an enormous curiosity and sudden concern about him. People with whom the Italian had lived for months now, sharing the mess, blankets and bombardment, and who had never bothered themselves about him, to the point of not even knowing his real name, asked him pointblank for his address, his profession in civilian life, and even discreetly interested themselves in his plans for the future.

All this had ended up by confusing the ideas the Italian had in his head, making him regret the good old times when the Scots grunted a kind of greeting at him in the morning, and didn't address another word to him, other than asking him for the salt or sugar at mess – those now fabled times of the 'probationary period.' As a consequence, the Italian examined his own conscience in turn and, alone, stretched out on his camp-bed, smoking one cigarette after another, beneath the affectionate and concerned gaze of his batman, passed his days rereading on the ceiling the story of his life with the battalion. He reproached himself for a lack of tact on some occasions and of resolution on others. He reproached himself with having been irritated for so long by the adjutant, until the night when, entering his room by mistake, he surprised him in pyjamas, kneeling on the floor, in front of his flag, in the act of praying to the Lord. From that moment on, he liked the adjutant, and had understood something of his shy, bashful, proud nature, fanatically dedicated to his duty.

At last, when the evening came in which the commanding officer sent to find him, the Italian felt himself overcome by a deep, melancholy feeling of peace.

'At last!' said the Italian, 'at last.'

He went to present himself to the colonel, who was quite ill at ease, so ill at ease that Pinto, at that moment, would have done anything to help him.

'John,' said the colonel. 'Will you have something to drink? There's a bottle of whisky on the table. Help yourself.'

'Thank you, sir,' said Lieutenant Pinto, forcing himself to smile.

'John,' said the colonel again, 'the moment has arrived when we have to part.'

'I know, sir,' said the Italian.

'Ah, so you know what's going on?' said the commanding officer with a sigh of relief. 'This way it's going to be much easier to say goodbye.'

'*Arrivederci*,' said Pinto, in Italian.

'*Arrivederci*,' the Scot repeated submissively. 'We're leaving and you haven't taught me to speak Italian. As you see, we really are incorrigible. We've always spoken English. It was easier, to be honest. And that's the reason I'll never learn a foreign language.'

'You'll have time to learn Arabic, now, sir,' said the Italian.

'Arabic?'

'I believe they speak Arabic in Palestine, as well as Hebrew,' said the Italian.

'You know this as well?' said the Scotsman, with a gesture of resignation. 'That we're going to Palestine? So we can't hide anything from you! It's true that you're an information officer, but you've made progress.'

'In your school, sir,' said the Italian. But he felt that it was all wrong, that they would never have arrived at the point of speaking to each other man to man, that it was impossible to 'communicate' with those men, except by conventional and approximate signs.

'It's been a pleasure having you with us,' said the colonel with a smile. His eyes were shining.

'An honour for me, sir,' said the Italian, 'to have been with the battalion.'

'It's a fine battalion,' said the colonel, raising his glass. 'It's a fine regiment.'

'Indeed, sir.'

'I hope to come back to Italy, once the war's over, with my

wife, and visit your family,' said the colonel. And then he said this extraordinary thing: 'The devil take it.'

And he repeated: 'The devil take it. I can't explain myself. Thank you for your assistance in the name of the battalion. That's it. Come in, lads!'

At this point, all the other officers at headquarters came in to greet the Italian and slap him on the back, and some of the younger ones embraced him. They presented him with two bottles of whisky, but the Italian wasn't able to take them away with him, because they were drunk on the spot, in a toast to the health of one and all.

The 6th Black Watch and the
Campaign in Italy

Trevor Royle

The military formation to which Gian Gaspare Napolitano was posted as a liaison officer was the 6th (Perthshire) Battalion of The Black Watch (Royal Highland Regiment), the senior Highland infantry regiment in the British Army with a record of service which stretches back to the eighteenth century. First created as Independent Companies of the Highland 'watch' to police the lawless upland areas of Scotland in the aftermath of the 1715 Jacobite rebellion, The Black Watch was raised officially as a regiment of the British Army in October 1739 at Aberfeldy in Perthshire. Its original army title was the 43rd Highlanders, but it was renumbered 42nd in 1751 following the reduction of the 42nd Foot (Oglethorpe's). From the outset the regiment wore the original dark black, green and blue government tartan; in time this led to it being known as *Am Freiceadan Dubh* or 'Black Watch' and the name stuck to become the formal title of the regiment. Another distinguishing feature is the red hackle worn in the Tam o'Shanter bonnet, a distinction which was awarded by King George III in 1795 to mark the regiment's bravery at Guildermaison during the British

Army's retreat towards the River Waal. At the time the 42nd formed part of an expeditionary force of British and Hessian regiments commanded by the Duke of York, King George III's second son, which had been dispatched to Flanders to support the Austrian army fighting against the armies of Revolutionary French. Although they and the other British regiments gave a good account of themselves under difficult circumstances, they were outnumbered three to one by the French army under the command of General Jean Houchard, and at one stage the British force was obliged to abandon its artillery. A series of exhausting marches and counter-marches dominated the campaign that was memorialised in the children's nursery song 'The Grand Old Duke of York', and following the surrender of Brussels and Antwerp to the French in July 1794 York's army was forced to withdraw to Britain.

In common with every other regiment in the British Army the history of The Black Watch has been one of constant change, not just of name but also of organisation, with operational battalions being raised and disbanded to meet the country's defence needs. In its latest manifestation, in March 2006, The Black Watch became the 3rd Battalion of The Royal Regiment of Scotland as part of a radical reorganisation of the structure of the British infantry which introduced a new large Scottish regiment with five regular and two territorial battalions representing the older Scottish regimental tradition. Two other dates stand out. Under a process begun in 1872 by the Secretary for War, Edward Cardwell, and finalised nine years later by his successor, Hugh Childers, the 42nd Highlanders were amalgamated with the 73rd (Perthshire) Foot to become the 1st and 2nd battalions of The Black Watch (Royal Highlanders). Driving the Cardwell/Childers reforms was the theory that one battalion would serve at home while the other was stationed abroad and would receive drafts and reliefs from the home-based battalion to keep it up to strength. As a result of those changes, regimental numbers were dropped and new names were adopted throughout the army but, as happens in every period of reform, the changes outraged older soldiers, who deplored the loss of cherished numbers and the introduction of what they held to be undignified titles.

There was further change in 1908, when the secretary for war, R. B. Haldane, introduced the Territorial Force, a second line service for home defence made up of part-time volunteers who were given basic military training and would be mobilised in time of war. With the exception of the foot guards, every infantry regiment in the British Army was allocated a number of Territorial Force battalions. The Black Watch contained four such formations, each one representing a part of the regiment's traditional recruiting area: 4th (City of Dundee), 5th (Dundee and Angus), 6th (Perthshire) and 7th (Fife). Each of the new Territorial battalions was based on earlier rifle volunteer corps, the 6th battalion's antecedent formation being the 1st Perthshire

Rifle Volunteers. Those units came into being in the middle of the nineteenth century, when Scotland was gripped by the 'Volunteer craze', a Victorian fancy for part-time soldiering which involved some gentle shooting practice and drills and, best of all, dressing up in turkey-cock uniforms. In Scotland the recruitment figures for the Rifle Volunteer units were twice the British average, a figure which was undoubtedly assisted by the creation of units with Highland affiliations, most of them in the Central Belt. With their panoply of kilts, tartan trews, ostrich feathers, ornate sporrans and pipe bands they were an irresistible attraction and everywhere men rushed to wear them. Most of those outlandish uniforms owed nothing to tradition but were invented by local colonels and they came to represent self-conscious nationalism or what the military historian John Keegan has described as 'a force for resistance against the creeping anglicisation of Scottish urban life'. However, there was more to volunteering than putting on fancy dress. Being a part-time soldier meant following an honourable calling: it was companionable, offered self-respect and produced steadiness of character, all important moral virtues in Presbyterian Scotland.

When the First World War broke out in August 1914, all four Black Watch Territorial Force battalions volunteered for service oversees, in their case fighting with the 51st (Highland) Division in France and Flanders. The 6th battalion had a particularly distinguished wartime career and earned the distinction of being awarded the Croix de Guerre for its support of French forces during the Second Battle of the Marne in the summer of 1918. During the fighting some 30,000 soldiers served in The Black Watch and by 1919, of their number 7,993 had been killed and around 20,000 had been wounded. As happens after every conflict, there was a rapid contraction of the armed forces and The Black Watch had to bear its share of the cuts. The first to suffer were the Territorial battalions when the 4th and 5th battalions were amalgamated to form the 4/5th Black Watch while the 6th and 7th became the 6/7th Black Watch. It was not until 1938, when another global conflict loomed, that they were 'separated from their Siamese embrace', as Eric and Andro Linklater put it in their regimental history, and returned to their earlier status to fight in another world war. On 2 September 1939 the 6th battalion assembled at Perth before moving to Aldershot in preparation for deployment in France as part of the 51st (Highland) Division. Due to the need to transfer men under the age of nineteen and the release of others, it was found necessary to reinforce the battalion with reservists from The Highland Light Infantry, a move that was not initially welcomed until it was discovered that the replacements quickly settled in, and on donning the regiment's tartan and red hackle became perfervid members of The Black Watch.

For everyone called up during that period, the opening rounds of the war did not produce grounds for any great confidence: in 1939 the British Army could put together only four divisions as an expeditionary force for Europe, six infantry and one armoured division in the Middle East, a field division and a brigade in India, two brigades in Malaya and a modest scattering of imperial garrisons elsewhere. Years of neglect and tolerance of old-fashioned equipment meant that the army was ill-prepared to meet the modern German forces in battle, and British industry was not geared to make good those deficiencies. Once again in the nation's history it seemed that Britain was going to war with the equipment and mentality of previous conflicts. Events in Poland quickly showed that Germany was a ruthless and powerful enemy: the country fell within eighteen days of the invasion, allowing the German leader Adolf Hitler to turn his attention to defeating France. While these events were unfolding The Black Watch consisted of two Regular battalions, the 1st battalion in Dover, the 2nd battalion in Palestine and four home-based Territorial battalions. Of these, the 4th and 6th battalions became part of the 51st (Highland) Division which was commanded by Major-General Victor Fortune, a Black Watch officer who had served with the 1st battalion in 1914 and had emerged from the war unscathed. The division crossed over to France in January, where it was strengthened by the introduction of three Regular battalions, one for each brigade. As a result, in March 1940, 1st Black Watch took the place of 6th Black Watch, which was transferred to the 4th Division, also in France. In a symbolic gesture the two Black Watch battalions (1st and 6th) made the changeover while on the march near Lille. It was a poignant moment: in June the 51st (Highland) Division was forced to surrender at St Valéry-en-Caux and the majority of its men went into captivity.

On 10 May, the period known as the 'phoney war' came to an end when German land and air forces attacked across the Low Countries as a prelude to invading France. The first Black Watch formation to see action was the 6th battalion, dug-in on the Seine Canal, to the north of Brussels, which it had been ordered to hold as a bridgehead to allow the 3rd Division to withdraw. Taken aback by the ferocity and speed of the German advance into Belgium, the British Expeditionary Force (BEF) had begun its long retreat back to the Channel ports and the 6th battalion was part of the process. On the night of 17 May the German attack reached the battalion's position, and its commanding officer Lieutenant-Colonel M. A. Carthew-Yorstoun received the order to start pulling back towards the Scheldt, following a route which would take them within 20 miles of the Fontenoy battlefield, the scene of the regiment's first fighting in Europe in 1745 during the War of the Austrian Succession. Other names nearby reminded older soldiers of the previous war – Ypres, Ploegsteert, Messines. It was a time of confusion and exhaustion. Covering up to 30 miles a day men almost fell asleep as they marched over the flat lands of Flanders, following the route along the Lys Canal from Petegem, south of Ghent, towards Coutrai. At Warneton Bridge, supported by armoured cars of 13th/18th Royal Hussars (Queen Mary's Own), the battalion put in a spirited counter-attack to deny the Germans the use of the bridge before blowing it up, but the final week of May was more about survival The final destination was the beachhead at Dunkirk which was reached on 1 June where, along with the rump of the BEF, they waited to be picked up in a number of small groups which had managed to make their way to the beaches and to safety.

On its return to Britain the battalion was stationed in the Isle of Wight before embarking on 15 months of training at various stations including Newbury, Camberley, Loch Fyne and Hawick before leaving for Algiers with 4th Division in March 1943 for the campaign against German and Italian Axis forces in North Africa. Serving in the First Army, the battalion fought in two major engagements – a night-attack at Sidi Medienne and the offensive against enemy positions at Enfidaville, which blocked the route to Tunis. The campaign ended on 11 May when all Axis resistance in North Africa came to an end.

The next stage of the war involved the capture of Sicily as a precursor to the invasion of peninsular Italy, a move which would lead to the final securing of the Mediterranean with its maritime routes, but even before the operation began, its planning was dogged by disagreements and acrimony. General George C. Marshall, the senior US commander, wanted to press ahead with plans for the invasion of northern Europe and to hit hard at Nazi Germany as the only way of winning the war. He forcefully told the Combined Chiefs of Staff that he did not want to have US forces being tied down in interminable operations in the Mediterranean, which he regarded as a strategic backwater. At the same time, the British prime minister, Winston Churchill, remained pre-occupied with attacking the 'soft underbelly of Europe' both as a means of engaging the Germans and knocking Italy out of the war. As described by his biographer, Martin Gilbert, Churchill's aim was 'to persuade the Americans to follow up the imminent conquest of Sicily by the invasion of Italy at least as far as Rome, and then to assist the Yugoslav, Greek and Albanian partisans in the liberation of the Balkans, by air support, arms and coastal landings by small Commando units'. At the Casablanca conference held in French Morocco between 14 and 24 January 1943, there was a marked divergence of opinion between the Allies over the choice of Sicily as the next target, with Sardinia or Corsica being preferred by some planners.

Following the capture of Sicily in August 1943, peninsular Italy was invaded by the British and US Allies the following month. At the same time the Italians surrendered, and while the Allies hesitated over the acceptance of the terms, the Germans moved 16 divisions into Italy to continue the war. These forces were to prove more than a handful for the Allies as they fought their way north from their landings at Salerno. Early in 1944 the Allied advance had been held up in the Liri Valley south of Rome, where the enemy resistance centred on the monastery at Monte Cassino, the mother-house of the Benedictine Order. It stood on high ground outside the town of the same name which had been razed to the ground and, being partially occupied by German forces, became the scene of fierce fighting in built-up areas. On 6 March 1944 the 6th battalion was committed to the fighting in Italy when it landed at Naples with 4th Division, having spent the interval between then and Tunis training in Algeria and Egypt. For the men under the command of Lieutenant-Colonel Brian Madden, it was a baptism of fire. Not only did they have to exchange the heat of Egypt for the sub-zero temperatures of a bitterly cold Italian winter, they also found themselves in the thick of the fighting for the strategically important position at Monte Cassino. Although they had been in continuous action in Tunis and had experience of engaging German forces, the war in Italy was dominated by constant enemy shellfire and hard skirmishing. In the hills above the River Garigliano the battalion held a bridgehead, leading what was described as a 'hole-and-corner life' with a good deal of aggressive patrolling.

There was some respite when 6th Black Watch was taken out of the line towards the end of the month, but the battalion was soon back in action again holding another bridgehead to the north-east of Cassino. Getting there involved a lengthy route march that was compared to passing the Lairig Ghru in the Cairngorms in the depths of winter. This was followed by a move into the sector of the town of Cassino where the battalion relieved 2nd Coldstream Guards. One Black Watch officer in the battalion, Archie Callander, found that he was taking over from his younger brother Ronnie who was serving in the foot-guards battalion being relieved. Due to the closeness of the enemy, there was no movement during the day and survival for the battalion meant placing a high premium on taking cover in the sangars which had been built in the ruins of the houses. Supplies had to be carried in and there was the constant danger of falling victim to enemy fire during these operations. One indication of the problems faced by the battalion comes from the statistic that British gunners fired up to 5,000 rounds of smoke shells to cover the carrying parties as they made their final approach to the British positions. Inevitably there were casualties. One of the most unusual involved Lance-Sergeant William Wilson of D Company, who had a direct family link on his mother's side to one of the first soldiers in the original Independent Companies. He first enlisted in 1908, served through the First World War, and when he was wounded by shellfire in Cassino he was 55 years old. His response to his predicament says much about the man and the regiment in which he served. As Sergeant Wilson was carried off to the casualty clearing station, he sent a message to his commanding officer asking to be excused for 'falling out without permission'.

Happily, he survived the incident and the war and returned to live in his native Aberdeen.

Following another short period out of the line, the battalion was ordered to attack enemy positions on the River Rapido, downstream of Cassino, and to make a bridgehead. In support of the attack a squadron of tanks from the Lothian and Border Horse was put under Madden's command and they set off in thick mist in the early morning of 13 May. By mid-morning they had reached their objective, but thick mist the following day hindered their progress and the companies began losing touch with one another – a potentially fatal mistake given that they were advancing into unknown territory. To prevent any mishaps, Madden ordered his men to form hollow squares, company by company, with the tanks in the middle, and to move off again. Hidden woods and German positions suddenly appeared in the mist-covered terrain and there was a succession of fire-fights before the battalion halted on a crest where the ground suddenly started falling away. The ensuing fire-fight was typical of the operations around Cassino – confused, relentless and intense, leaving the battalion with 240 casualties killed or wounded before Polish forces finally fought their way into Monte Cassino and flew their national flag above the ruins of the monastery on 17 May. During this period the battalion was reinforced by soldiers from The Transvaal Scottish, one of The Black Watch's affiliated regiments which was formed at the conclusion of the Boer War in 1902.

The fall of Monte Cassino opened up access to the valley of the River Liri and the coastal littoral, thus allowing the Allied infantry and armoured divisions to push north-east towards Rome. At the same time, on 23 May, US VI Corps broke out of the Anzio beachhead, having been bogged down there after the initial landings on 22 January. Rome fell to the US Fifth Army on 5 June and the Germans began a fighting retreat towards the Pisa–Rimini line, an operation in which the 6th battalion played a full role. They also took part in the next phase of the Allied advance towards the Gothic Line in the Appenines to the north of Florence, stretching from Carrara in the west to Pesaro on the Adriatic. On 15 July the Allies had reached the River Arno where they halted and regrouped. A requirement for additional forces for the invasion of the south of France meant that the Allies lost the French Expeditionary Corps, whose north African troops had excelled in mountain warfare, and the US VI Corps. Their places were taken by the Brazilian Corps of 25,000 soldiers – Brazil had declared war on the Axis powers on 22 August 1942 – but as they had not yet been tested in battle the Allied advance had perforce to be slowed down.

On 25 August the Allies began their attack on the Gothic line with the US Fifth Army on the left flank and the British Eighth Army on the right flank. Under the command of General Sir Oliver Leese, the British attacked across the River Foglia with with V Corps on the left, I Canadian Corps in the centre and II Polish Corps on the right. The 6th battalion was heavily involved in the fighting which took the 4th Infantry Division from Foligno to Cesena and Forlì to the north-west of Rimini. It was at this stage in the campaign that Napolitano joined 6th Black Watch as a liaison officer. Although his own account makes it clear that he received a cautious welcome and was accorded all the formalities due to an army officer, it cannot have been an easy transition. At the time the British Army did not have a particularly high opinion of the fighting qualities of Italian soldiers, and the victories in North Africa and Sicily had built up a feeling that bordered on contempt. (A contemporary army joke says it all: 'How many gears does an Italian tank possess? Four in reverse and one forward in case the enemy attacks from the rear.') The men of 6th Black Watch were probably no different. At the end of the campaign in North Africa they had been responsible for guarding enemy prisoners in a camp near Sousse, and Madden's war history makes it clear that his men quickly made differences between the Italians and the Germans.

Guarding the POWs was not uninteresting psychologically. The Germans were naturally completely disciplined and efficient, the Italians dirty and unhygienic. The Germans had great contempt for the Italians, the Italians considerable fear of the Germans.

We had to keep them separate. It was too easy. We gave the Germans wire and told them to erect a barricade between themselves and the Italians. It was up in no time – they weren't going to mix with Mussolini's warriors. We gave the Italians wire and a similar order. Up went the barricades again – anything to make themselves safe from their allies.

During this period a number of Italian prisoners-of-war were employed by the battalion in a variety of administrative tasks, but this practice had to be discouraged as, according to Madden, the Jocks in the battalion 'just sat back and let the Italians do all the work, which was extremely bad for them'.

By the time of Napolitano's arrival, the Italian campaign was being run down, with many formations being reduced in strength to provide battlefield replacements for the fighting in north-west Europe following the D-Day invasion at the beginning of June. In the course of July the battalion lost seven commanding officers in succession, including Madden, who was wounded in July during the advance to Florence and was replaced by Major G. McP. Smith. During the same period it was consistently short of around 100 men and had to reduce its rifle companies from four to three, with D Company being disbanded. Despite the lack of men and replacements, the fighting was consistently heavy and the period described in Napolitano's narrative was as exacting as any other in the Italian campaign. Having spent part of August in Foligno near Lake Trasimene where the billets were a former mental hospital, the battalion moved up to its concentration area at Pesaro in preparation for its first objective, forcing a bridgehead over the River Marano at Ospedaletto. The heavy rains mentioned by Napolitano and stubborn German resistance at Coriano meant that the attack did not materialise until 14 September, when 6th Black Watch went into the attack with 2nd Royal West Kents in the centre and 2nd Royal Fusiliers on the left. Following a 'short, sharp action', the position was taken, despite the presence of German tanks, including a much-feared Tiger, a 57-ton monster equipped with the excellent 88-mm anti-armour gun.

The next stage of the campaign saw 6th Black Watch involved in the fighting for the Rimini gap, the area between the mountains and the sea which allowed the advancing allied armies to move on Forlì and Faenza. This involved them in the two final major operations of the campaign: the battle for Cesena and the Savio bridgehead, which was fought between 20 and 23 October, and the advance on Forlì in the middle of November. Napolitano calls them battles that would figure in the history of The Black Watch, and he was right to give them that distinction. In the first action, the attack on Cesena, there were problems even before the operation began, when the Germans opened concentrated fire on an S-bend in the river as C Company was passing through the area. As a result two officers and three soldiers were killed, one of the casualties being Major Archie Callander, whom Madden described as 'a very long-standing member of the battalion and yet another very much beloved friend'. The incident is also mentioned by Napoli-tano in the chapter dealing with the battalion's padre, Captain Joseph Grant. Having established a bridgehead, the battalion found itself involved in heavy fighting with the Germans, the main problem being to protect their positions and the supply routes to them. During the battle, A Company had unexpected good fortune when they cap-tured a German ration party and confiscated their holdings. It was not until 24 October that the enemy pulled out of Cesena and revealed themselves to be the elite 1st Parachute Division, which had fought against 6th Black Watch earlier in the campaign at Cassino.

For the next battle, the advance towards Forlì on 7 November, the battalion was supported by the tanks of the North Irish Horse, with whom they had fought in North Africa at Djebel Rmel. This involved them in fighting in a built-up area as they moved through Forlì, where they met determined resistance in the shape of mortar and Spandau machine-gun fire. The whole operation lasted four days. During the attack the supporting artillery fired 280 rounds of assorted ammunition in a fifteen-minute period. Casualties were limited to 70 killed or wounded, and although the battle was described as a small-scale affair, it epitomised the type of fighting which the battalion experienced in the final days of the Italian campaign. As Madden put it, the advance might have seemed 'nothing, but anyone who has tried street-fighting knows the sort of progress that can be expected in a day against a determined enemy'. By mid-December the Eighth Army had reached the River Senio, and this proved to be the limit of its advance in 1944. With the onset of heavy winter weather, Field Marshal Sir Harold Alexander, Commander-in-Chief Mediterranean, decided to call a halt to offensive operations until the following spring.

As a result of the draw-down in the Allies' operations the 4th Infantry Division, including 6th Black Watch was ordered out of the line and sent south to Taranto in preparation for a new move to what was widely thought to be Palestine for a period of training in river crossings. However, when they arrived at the port they found that they were being diverted to Greece to reinforce the British forces which had been deployed to intervene in the civil war in the aftermath of the German withdrawal in the autumn of 1944. It was a thankless task as the British forces had to act in support of the authorities against an insurrection mounted ELAS, the Communist Party's well-organised military wing. The battalion was deployed first in Athens and then in the more remote country areas around Mount Parnassus. As happens in any civil war, the troops charged with attempting to hold the peace had a torrid time, and the 6th battalion suffered a number of casualties during their deployment which did not end until 8 June 1946, the date of the battalion's final parade in Athens. After the war came the inevitable defence cutbacks and the 6th battalion renewed its amalgamation with the 7th battalion to become 6/7th Black Watch, which remained in being until 1967 when, under a radical change to the Territorial Army, it became part of a new Scottish Territorial regiment, the 51st Highland Volunteers. In 2006, as part of the restructuring of the British infantry, the Highland Volunteers became part of 8th Battalion, The Royal Regiment of Scotland.

In writing about his experiences with 6th Black Watch, Napolitano quickly and astutely grasped the dynamics of soldiering in a Highland Territorial infantry battalion of that period. At that stage in the war when he became a liaison officer, the complexion of the battalion had changed dramatically and five years of warfare in Europe and North Africa had left their mark on its soldiers. The battalion was no longer composed principally of part-time Territorials who had enjoyed weekend soldiering in the breezy pre-war years; the need to replace battlefield casualties meant that regulars served alongside volunteers, Englishmen became temporary Jocks and in action the men wore standard British battledress. (To the regret of the regiment, a War Office order in 1940 forbade the use of kilts, although they were worn on ceremonial occasions throughout the war.)

Just as Napolitano introduced himself in his narrative as Lieutenant Pinto, so too did he mostly use fictional names for the main personalities whom he describes so well and so accurately. The commanding officer who took the battalion to Italy was Lieutenant-Colonel Brian Madden, a regular soldier who had joined The Black Watch as a subaltern in August 1928 and had served as the adjutant of the 2nd battalion between 1934 and 1937. Invalided out of the army in September 1938, he rejoined a year later on the outbreak of hostilities with Germany and was appointed commanding officer of the 6th battalion in April 1943. At the conclusion of the war he served with 5th Black Watch and commanded 1st Gordon Highlanders for a short period before returning to the 6th battalion in March 1946, commanding it until its disbandment three months later. As the battalion had seven commanding officers during the Italian campaign the likelihood is that Napolitano's creation is a composite character based on those whom he knew – Major G. McP. Smith was in command when he joined the battalion. The second-in-command in August 1944 was Major Lord Douglas Gordon, another career officer, who had joined The Black Watch as a subaltern in January 1937 and had gone on to serve with the 2nd battalion in Palestine. He took over command of the 6th battalion from Madden and served as a staff officer in the post-war Regular Army; in Napolitano's narrative he is called Lord Dix. Other easily recognised personalities include the battalion's padre, the Revd Joseph Grant, who served with 6th Black Watch throughout the war. Born at Ballater in Aberdeenshire on 26 December 1904, Grant was educated at Robert Gordon's College and the University of Aberdeen and was ordained and inducted at Rhynie in 1931 before taking over the charge of Cromdale six years later. In 1945 he was awarded the Military Cross and he won a lasting reputation within The Black Watch for his unstinting work in retrieving battlefield casualties for burial. He retired from the ministry in 1971 and died on 25 July 1990.

Whatever their original provenance though, all the personalities in Napolitano's narrative are typical of the kind of British soldier – volunteer and professional alike – who gave sterling service to the country, fighting in distinguished Territorial battalions such as 6th Black Watch during its long march from France in 1940, through north Africa to Italy and finally to Greece, where it ended its war.

Edinburgh/Angus, February 2007

Further reading

Eric and Andro Linklater, *The Black Watch: the history of the Royal Highland Regiment*. London: Barrie & Jenkins, 1977.

B. J. G. Madden, *A History of the 6th Battalion The Black Watch, Royal Highland Regiment 1939–45*. Perth: D. Leslie, 1948.

Trevor Royle, *The Black Watch: A Concise History*. Edinburgh: Mainstream, 2006.

Note on the text

The sixteen episodes that make up *To War with The Black Watch* have a surprisingly complex textual history. The complexities reflect both the Italian political situation on first publication, at the end of the Second World War, and the author's repeated revisions of his material.

Most of the stories in *To War with The Black Watch* were published in the Rome newspaper, *Libera Stampa*, between August and December 1945. *Libera Stampa* was a double-sided broadsheet, printed on poor-quality paper. Despite the post-war austerities – the first story competed for space with news that Shanghai was once more under Chinese control; serious food shortages at home; intimidation and coercion in the Bulgarian elections; and the sinking of 325 Japanese naval vessels by the Americans – *Libera Stampa* found a regular place for fiction. So, Napolitano's lightly fictionalised accounts of his experiences with The Black Watch would eventually be succeeded by the work of others, including the author's exact contemporary, the distinguished novelist Alberto Moravia, who published in the issue of 16 December 1945.

Napolitano's stories originally appeared at weekly intervals, under the pen-name of 'Nino Santini', a combination of a diminutive form of the author's Christian name (Gian = Giovanni = Giovannino = Nino) and Santini (the maiden name of his mother, Geltrude). From the second episode onwards, the title *In guerra con gli scozzesi* (*To War with the Scots*) appeared over the individual titles. The tales appeared in the following order, sometimes with different titles:

19 August: *Un posto a mensa* – A place in the mess
(originally: *Ci sono milioni di britannici che non si sentono europei* – There are millions of British who don't feel themselves Europeans)

26 August: *A titolo personale* – In a personal capacity
(originally: *Il Dottore non ama il sangue* – The doctor doesn't like blood)

2 September: Buying provisions – *Alla spesa viveri*
(originally: *L'ufficiale veniva da Bulavayo* – The officer comes from Bulawayo)

9 September: *Le bestemmie del Quartiermastro* – The Quartermaster's cursing
(originally: *Profano e sacro* – Profane and sacred)

16 September: *Lo scandalo del vino* – The wine scandal
(originally: *Inchiesta sul vino* – Enquiry into the wine)

23 September: *Domenica di mattina* – Sunday morning)

30 September: *Dialogo nella buca* – Conversation in a dug-out

7 October: *Padre Grant* – Padre Grant

14 October: *Il battaglione si diverte* – The battalion enjoys itself

21 October: *Jimmy Mc Donald* – Jimmy McDonald

28 October: *Una storia di borghesi* – A story about civilians

4 November: *Io appartengo a Glasgow* – I belong to Glesca

11 November: *Il passaggio del Savio* – Crossing the Savio (originally: *Il passaggio del Senio* – Crossing the Senio)

18 November: *Il battaglione se ne va* – The battalion moves off

Four further episodes, published in *Libera Stampa* in 1945, detailed Lieut. Pinto's experiences with an Indian battalion: 'Il battaglione indiano Tika' (25 November); 'Medico di Madras' (2 December); 'Dimmi come mangi' (9 December); 'Subedar Ibrahim' (16 December).

A number of the stories in *To War with The Black Watch* were published at later dates. So, 'I belong to Glasgow' appeared, in a revised but not final form, in *Corriere di Milano* on 27 June 1948. Both 'Sixteen crosses' (*Sedici croci*) and 'The empirical major' (*L'empirico maggiore*) first appeared, along with revised versions of other stories, in the magazine *Cronache* in 1954; an abbreviated version of the latter story had originally been incorporated into *Il Dottore non ama il sangue* (26 August 1945), and appeared in *Cronache* as *Il caso del maggiore Elms*, or 'The Case of Major Elms'. The first collected version of the stories, with three of

171

the four Indian episodes, appeared under the title *In guerra con gli scozzesi* (Palermo: Sellerio, 1986).

The original typescripts of the stories in the versions published in *Libera Stampa*, heavily revised in Napolitano's own hand, along with later revisions in typescript – some edited by the author's wife, the translator, Maria Martone, are currently held in the Gian Gaspare Napolitano archive in the Biblioteca Statale Antonio Baldini, Rome. The archive was recently donated to the library by the author's daughter, Giovanna Napolitano. I am grateful to the Director of the Biblioteca Statale Antonio Baldini, Dott.ssa Silvia De Vincentiis, and her courteous and helpful staff, as well as to Signora Napolitano, for their assistance in locating the various versions of the stories in the as yet uncatalogued archive. I am also grateful to the Director and staff of the Archivio Capitolino, Rome, which holds a complete run of the relevant issues of *Libera Stampa*.

ICR, 7 February 2007

Extract from a letter written by Gian Gaspare Napolitano, describing his experiences in the early days of his service with The Black Watch

25 September 1944

. . . I live with a British unit, about which I can give you no further information. I get on well with them, very well in fact. I'm the only Italian officer, and living completely apart from all the other officers of the Italian Liberation Corps. The majority of the officers in the unit are Scottish; they're good people, kind, discreet, reserved, and excellent company . . .

It's an old British tradition never to ask you anything about yourself; and to study you in depth before deciding what kind of work you might be given to do. So much for my work. As far as the rest is concerned, things are going equally well. I mean in terms of health, food, tobacco. But you know that I'm not over sensitive about all these small comforts; I appreciate them for what they're worth and no more. The important thing rather is that I'm fine here, in good spirits, even though I'm completely and utterly by myself. I haven't seen an Italian paper since I left Rome. Yet even that doesn't bother me a bit. In fact, looking at it in one way, I feel all the better for it. I'm completely contented, and only miss news of all those who are dear to me. You know I've always loved army life, and the company of soldiers. So, this is a wonderful experience for me, despite the fact that it's taking place in the most wretched circumstances for my country. Everyone is extremely considerate, even in this regard, or rather particularly in this regard. The weather's still mild and agreeable. I'm on high ground here and can see hills and fields, and in the distance [censured*]. The countryside is beautiful and taking everything into consideration hasn't suffered much from the war. The towns and villages, and farmhouses, on the other hand, have taken a beating, often a very bad one . . .

* A note adds that the word censured is 'Rimini' or 'Riccione'

Translated Ian Campbell Ross

Source: Napolitano Archive, Biblioteca Statale Antonio Baldini, Rome.

Rome, 29/6/45

As Intelligence Officer of the Battalion to which Gian
Gaspare Napolitano was attached as I[ntelligence] L[iaison]
O[fficer] I would like to pay some little tribute to his valued
assistance.

In Nov. 1943 Gian joined the Battalion and within a very
few days had rendered us valuable assistance in many directions.

The information which he sought unceasingly from civilian sources proved invaluable in the location of enemy
booby-traps, mine fields and tunnels in the river banks by
which German patrols had frequently gained access to our
lines, information which was to prove an important factor in
the ultimate capture of the River Montone line.

Later in the Battle of Faenza and again in the Central
Sector we were greatly indebted to Gian for the difficult and
trying task of evacuating refugees and civilian wounded from

the front line, often under conditions of extreme danger, for the interrogation of prisoners and the thousand and one tasks that fall to the lot of an I.O.

Throughout this period Gian had become so much a member of the Battalion that it was with sincere regret that we learned he was to return to civil life, but he can be assured of a hearty welcome in the homes and clubs of the Bn. Officers should he at some future date come to England and enable us to return some measure of the hospitality he has extended to many of us.

Raymond E. Legge, Capt.

Source: Napolitano Archive, Biblioteca Statale Antonio Baldini, Rome.

Letter by the Revd Joseph Grant (1904–90), Church of Scotland
Minister and Chaplain, 6th Battalion, The Black Watch (Italian
original)

Cara [. . .], La ringrazio di avermi cortesemente mandato
la copia dell'articolo scritto da Gian Gaspare Napolitano che
riguarda la nostra visita a Firenze verso la fine del 1944.

Io ricevetti una lettera che mi diceva che lui stava morendo
e che mi chiedeva se avessi potuto mandargli una breve nota
che avesse potuto essergli di conforto. Gli scrissi esprimendo
la mia fiducia che lo spirito del suo calmo coraggio che aveva
sempre dimostrato in Guerra gli sarebbe stato di aiuto nelle
sue ore di sofferenza.

Devo scusarmi per aver tardato tanto a rispondere, ma,
data la mia ignoranza dell'italiano, ho mandato la lettera al
dipartimento italiano all'Università di Aberding [sic]; mi
promisero una traduzione ma, essendo stati molto occupati
hanno impiegato molto tempo, ed io l'ho ricevuta solo due
giorni fa.

Come lei dice John, come tutti noi lo chiamavamo, era una

giusta e buona persona. Ricordo perfettamente la sua cultura, la sua pazienza ed il suo tono signorile. Mi sono assai spesso chiesto quanto doveva averlo appenato la vista del suo bel paese distrutto dalla Guerra, e mi rallegro che abbia vissuto tanto a lungo per vederlo rimesso in piedi. Per quanto riguarda il breve scritto che lui mi ha dedicato, temo che mi abbia dipinto con colori troppo splendenti e, le assicuro, molto immeritati. Se mi sentirò depresso penserò a quello scritto perchè mi dia una migliore opinione di me stesso.

Se il suo libro non è stato ancora pubblicato, mi chiedo se non posso dare qualche suggerimento per quello che mi riguarda, in due punti dell'articolo. Il traduttore scrive: 'La situazione al nostro arrivo a Riccione è ambigua, riguarda la morte di Callander'. Noi naturalmente sapevamo della sua morte, a seguito di ferite. Posso suggerire che l'ambiguità possa essere evitata con una variazione nel testo nel punto che comincia 'loro debono fermarsi a Riccione per rendere l'ultimo omaggio ad Archie Callander, un maggiore che era morto in seguito a ferite due giorni prima, e che era stato seppellito nel cimitero alleato, situato dietro l'ospedale'.

L'ultimo paragrafo si presta ad una interpretazione errata e può essere che John abbia confuso Archie con un altro scozzese. Archie preveniva dal Sud della Scozia, non da questo distretto del Nord dove vivo io, e suggerirei il senso di quest'ultimo paragrafo 'come farò a dirlo a sua madre?', pronunziato a bassa voce, fissando intensamente la strada . . .: 'I Callander sono una delle più importanti famiglie del

Midlothian e Archie era un abile sportivo e immagino le sue lotte alla pesca del salmone nel Tweed. Quando l'acqua è chiara si possono vedere le pietre sul letto del fiume, e le belle creature argentee stese sul fondo'. Egli seguita a fissare la strada e poi, di colpo sorrido dicendo: 'Ero tornato in Scozia'.

Un'ultima cosa: alla pagina uno del testo bisogna correggere il nome di John Grant che è invece Joseph Grant. Spero vorrà perdonarmi di questo breve commento, ma penso che a John farebbe piacere questa accuratezza. La pubblicazione del Suo libro, ne sono sicuro, procurerà a Lei un profondo e durevole piacere.

La ringrazio di nuovo per aver preso la pena di mandarmi questo scritto. Ricordo John con affetto, e Le mando i miei migliori auguri, e possa Dio benedire l'Italia, per me ricordo indelebile.

Suo, sinceramente,

    [F.to] Joseph Grant

Archie aveva capelli bruni e occhi scuri. Nel testo si legge: 'L'italiano lo ricorda per i suoi occhi chiari e il suo sorriso infantile e la sua volontà di rimanere nell'esercito dopo la guerra e diventare soldato di carriera'.

Source: Napolitano Archive, Biblioteca Statale Antonio Baldini, Rome.

Letter by the Revd Joseph Grant (1904–90), Church of Scotland
Minister and Chaplain, 6th Battalion, The Black Watch

Dear [. . .],

Thank you for having so kindly sent me the copy of the article
written by Gian Gaspare Napolitano, concerning our visit to
Florence towards the end of 1944.

I received a letter telling me he was dying and asking if I
could send him a short note that might be of comfort to him.
I wrote to him, expressing my confidence that the spirit of
the calm courage he had always shown in battle would be of
help to him in his hours of suffering.

I must apologise for having taken so long to reply but not
knowing Italian I sent the letter to the Italian department at
Aberdeen University; they promised me a translation but,
being very busy, took a long time over it, and I only received
it two days ago.

As you say, John, as we all called him, was a just and a good
person. I remember perfectly his erudition, his patience, and
his refined gentlemanly manner. I often asked myself how

much it must have pained him to see his beautiful country destroyed by war, and I'm glad he lived long enough to see it firmly back on its feet. As far as the brief account he gave of myself, I'm afraid he painted me in colours that are too splendid and, I assure you, quite unmerited. If I ever feel depressed, I shall think of that piece because it will give me a better opinion of myself.

If his book hasn't been published yet, I wonder whether I might make some suggestions on a couple of points concerning myself. The translator writes: 'The situation when we arrived at Riccione was uncertain, so far as Callander's death was concerned.' Naturally, we knew he had died, as a result of his wounds. Can I suggest that the ambiguity could be avoided by changing the text at the point that begins: 'they have to stop at Riccione to pay their last respects to Archie Callander, a major who had died of his wounds two days earlier, and who had been buried in the allied cemetery, situated behind the hospital.'

The last sentence lends itself to misinterpretation and it may have been that John confused Archie with another Scotsman. Archie came from the south of Scotland, not from this district in the north where I live, and I'd suggest that the last sentence – 'how will I tell his mother?' – spoken in a low voice, his eyes fixed on the road . . . read 'The Callanders are one of the most important families in Midlothian and Archie was a talented sportsman and I can imagine his struggles salmon-fishing in the Tweed. When the water is clear, you can see the stones on the river-bed, and the beautiful silver creatures lying on the bottom'. He continued to stare at the road and then, suddenly smiling, said, "I was back in Scotland".'

One last thing: on page one of the text the name John Grant should be corrected to read Joseph Grant. I hope you'll forgive these few comments, but I think that John would have liked this accuracy. I'm sure the publication of his book will give you a deep and lasting pleasure.

Thank you again for having taken the trouble to send me the work. I remember John with affection, and send him my best wishes, and may God bless Italy – an indelible memory for me.

Yours sincerely,
        [signed] Joseph Grant

Archie had brown hair and dark eyes. The text has 'The Italian remembers his pale eyes and his childlike smile and his wish to remain in the army after the war and become a career officer.'

Translated Ian Campbell Ross

BIRLINN LTD (incorporating John Donald and Polygon) is one of Scotland's leading publishers with over four hundred titles in print. Should you wish to be put on our catalogue mailing list **contact**:

Catalogue Request
Birlinn Ltd
West Newington House
10 Newington Road
Edinburgh EH9 1QS
Scotland, UK

Tel: + 44 (0) 131 668 4371
Fax: + 44 (0) 131 668 4466
e-mail: info@birlinn.co.uk

Postage and packing is free within the UK. For overseas orders, postage and packing (airmail) will be charged at 30% of the total order value.

For more information, or to order online, visit our website at **www.birlinn.co.uk**

Birlinn *Limited*
IMPRINTS: JOHN DONALD · POLYGON